Beyond A Jo

A Comedy

Derek Benfield

Samuel French — London
New York — Sydney — Toronto — Hollywood

BEYOND A JOKE

First presented by Newpalm Productions on a national tour following a summer season at The Shanklin Theatre, Isle of Wight, which opened on July 2nd 1979 with the following cast of characters:

Jane	Honor Shepherd
Andrew	Arthur Lowe
Geoff	Peter Greene
Sally	Annette Woollett
Sarah	Joan Cooper
Vicar	Vyvian Hall
Audrey	Jane Elliott
Edgar	Brian Tully

The play directed by Christopher Bond
Setting by Kenneth Turner

The action takes place in the drawing-room and part of the garden of Andrew and Jane's detached house in the country
It is summertime and the going is easy

ACT I
    SCENE 1   Friday evening
    SCENE 2   Saturday morning

ACT II
    SCENE 1   A few seconds later
    SCENE 2   After lunch the same day

Time—the present

ACT I

Scene 1

The drawing-room and part of the garden of Andrew and Jane's detached house in the country. A Friday evening in summer: the sun is shining

In the drawing-room an archway leads out into the hall and the rest of the house, and there is a cupboard DR *with a small armchair in front of it. A two-seater sofa stands centrally, with a coffee table below it and a well-stocked drinks table above it. Against the wall immediately above the sofa is a handsome desk with a telephone on it and bookshelves around it. The furniture and decoration show the presence of both money and good taste. There is a window, with practical curtains, in the central wall with a window seat inside. An open glass door above the window leads out to the garden, where there is a splendid red brick wall and an abundance of shrubs and bright flowers. There is a way off which leads "up the garden" and round to the front of the house, and another which leads "down the garden" and to the pond. A wooden seat stands in the middle of the garden with a table below it, and there is a garden chair* DC. *A ladder is in position against the side of the house, with a bucket of water at its foot. The whole atmosphere is of a dreamy, peaceful, bee-buzzing English country garden. (See plan of set, page 81)*

Jane comes into the garden from the front of the house, putting on her rubber kitchen gloves. She is an attractive woman of about forty-seven, wearing slacks and a shirt. She takes a wash-leather out of the bucket, squeezes out the surplus water and looks apprehensively up the ladder. Then she starts to climb, carefully and not too confidently

Andrew's voice is heard from the hall

Andrew (*off*) Jane! Jane!

Oblivious, Jane continues to climb slowly

Andrew walks in from the hall into the drawing-room. He has just got home from work in the City. He is a pleasant, relaxed man in his middle-fifties. He wears a business suit and carries the evening paper and a brief-case. He puts them down and looks about. He sees the ladder outside, looks puzzled and goes out into the garden. He sees Jane going up the ladder and watches her for a moment in silence

(*Eventually*) Jane!

Jane reacts and nearly falls

What on earth are you doing up there?

Jane Really, Andrew! Creeping up and surprising me like that. I might have fallen off.

Andrew I didn't expect to find you up a ladder.

Jane Why not?

Andrew Well, I don't usually come home on a Friday night and find you up a ladder. Not what I'm used to.

Jane (*looking up at the windows*) You shouldn't get so set in your ways.

A brief pause

Andrew Any special reason?

Jane What?

Andrew Look, I can't talk to you up there. For heaven's sake come down.

Jane I'm not sure if I can.

Andrew Oh, my God! (*He starts to go inside*)

Jane Where are you going?

Andrew To call the Fire Brigade.

Jane Darling. I'm only up a ladder.

Andrew Long way down.

Jane Don't be silly. I'm only halfway up.

Andrew So if you fall you'll only break *half* a leg, is that it? You know perfectly well that in this house someone has only to trip over the edge of the carpet and they seem to break their neck.

Jane slips

Jane Ooh!

Andrew Are you all right?

Jane Yes. I think so.

Andrew wanders to the garden chair

Andrew That's all I need. Come home from work and find my wife lying dead in the garden.

Jane I'm not dead *yet*.

Andrew You're not *down* yet, either. (*He sits on the garden chair*) What on earth were you doing?

Jane I was going to clean the windows.

Andrew What for?

Jane Because the garden looks so lovely from our bedroom window at this time of the year. (*Romantically*) All the phlox and hollyhocks, and those nice blue flowers like bells all along the edge . . .

Andrew Darling . . .

Jane Yes?

Andrew Wouldn't it have been easier to get a window-cleaner?

Jane (*ominously*) Ah. Well . . .

Andrew looks apprehensive

Andrew Don't tell me something's happened to the window-cleaner?

Jane He wouldn't come.

Andrew Why not?
Jane Well—I suppose he must have *heard.*
Andrew Heard?
Jane About what happened to the last one.
Andrew Oh, no . . .
Jane Oh, yes! I think I'll try to come down now.

Andrew goes to the foot of the ladder

Andrew Wait a minute! I'll come up and help you.
Jane Then we'd *both* fall.
Andrew If we're going to go—let's go together!
Jane Don't be silly, Andrew. It's only a few steps.
Andrew Rungs, darling.
Jane Sorry?
Andrew Rungs in ladders. Steps in stairs.
Jane Oh, yes. (*She starts to come down*)
Andrew Hang on! I'll get some cushions in case you fall.
Jane I'm half-way down already.
Andrew (*admiringly*) Good lord. So you are. How splendid!

She reaches the ground and he embraces her delightedly

There! You made it! I'm proud of you.
Jane (*laughing*) I'm not a sherpa coming down from Everest, you know.
Andrew It's just as dangerous. With the track record in this house you
   need a seat belt to go to the lavatory. (*He sits on the garden seat*) How
   on earth did he find out?
Jane Who?
Andrew The new window-cleaner. About the old one.
Jane Oh, you know how people talk. I expect he heard it on the grapevine.
   (*She takes off her rubber gloves*)
Andrew I didn't know window-cleaners had grapevines.
Jane You could hardly expect his wife not to mention it. If your husband
   falls off a ladder and breaks his neck, it's bound to come up in the
   conversation.
Andrew Well, it wasn't *my* fault. I was at work. Can't spend all day
   holding ladders for window-cleaners.
Jane (*thoughtfully*) I expect they've put a secret sign on the gatepost.

Andrew looks at her bemusedly

Like those old tramps in Saltash, do you remember? They always
knew where to go for bread-and-jam and fresh tea.
Andrew What are you talking about?
Jane I expect that's how they knew not to come *here* . . .
Andrew Tramps?
Jane Window-cleaners.
Andrew You mean there's some sort of squiggle on our gate somewhere
   that means "Stay away if you want to stay alive"?

Jane Wouldn't be surprised.
Andrew Well, I think that's very unfair. Sam was the only window-cleaner who ever died in this house. The only one! That won't get us into the *Guinness Book of Records*, will it?
Jane Not if you don't include the *others*.

Andrew sighs regretfully

Andrew Well, it's not my fault. We've just got an unlucky house. (*He tries to cheer up*) Come on—I want a drink.

They go into the house. Andrew sees to the drinks

Gin and tonic for you?
Jane H'm. Lovely. (*She glances at the evening paper that Andrew brought in with him*) By the way—Sylvia rang this morning.
Andrew Sylvia?
Jane Of Sylvia and George.
Andrew Oh, yes?
Jane They were coming to dinner tomorrow.
Andrew Were they?
Jane You'd forgotten.
Andrew Completely.
Jane Well, it doesn't matter because they've changed their minds and now they're not.
Andrew Well, I think that's rather rude. (*He hands her a drink*) There you are.
Jane Thank you, darling.

He goes back to see to his own drink

Andrew Why not?
Jane They can't get a baby-sitter. (*She sits on the window-seat with the newspaper*)
Andrew What on earth do they want with a baby-sitter? They've only got one child and he works in the Foreign Office.
Jane Dogs.
Andrew Ah. Dog-sitter. That's never bothered them before.
Jane No. I thought it was a pretty feeble excuse.
Andrew You think they were *looking* for an excuse?
Jane Well, I asked them to change to *next* Saturday. Or the following Wednesday, Friday or Sunday.
Andrew And they couldn't manage *any* of those?
Jane Fully booked.
Andrew Don't be silly, darling. Sylvia and George are never fully booked. They only go out twice a year. They're terrified of being out the night there's something good on television. (*He sits on the sofa*)
Jane Perhaps they didn't *want* to come.

He looks at her

Andrew Good lord. You don't suppose they . . .? Oh, no, they couldn't have done, could they?

Jane Got to know about our wretched accidents?

Andrew It's bound to put people off a bit if they do find out. You haven't mentioned any of them to Sylvia?

Jane looks a little guilty

Jane Well—I might have mentioned one or two.

Andrew Well, there you are. That's why they're not coming to dinner.

Jane I didn't think.

Andrew (*gently*) Look, darling, even one or two fatal accidents are bound to tip the balance when it comes to dinner parties. I expect Sylvia has got the idea that we're accident-prone.

Jane Well, you can't blame her. It *is* beginning to look like it.

Andrew So she probably thinks that if she brings George to dinner he'll choke on an avocado pear.

Jane Well, I'm not going to leave the stones in, am I?

Andrew relaxes on the sofa with his drink. He sighs heavily

Andrew It is a bit depressing, isn't it?

Jane You must try not to think about it. (*She glances idly through the evening paper*)

Andrew Not very easy. I mean, after all, how many is it now? Five?

Jane Six.

Andrew Six? Good lord. Becoming embarrassing.

Jane Darling, you mustn't worry. It could happen to anybody.

Andrew Yes, but it *has* happened to us! I'm afraid to ask anyone home for a drink in case something happens to them.

Jane Well, at least it hasn't happened to any of our friends.

Andrew No. That's some consolation. (*Thoughtfully*) Good lord. Six. . . .

She goes and sits next to him, puts down the newspaper and kisses him cosily on the top of the head

That's very nice. Any special reason?

Jane No. Just felt like it.

Andrew I see.

A cosy pause—both thinking

I suppose Geoff's coming for the week-end again?

Jane smiles at the slight disapproval in his voice

Jane He hasn't said not.

Andrew Becoming a bit of a habit.

Jane H'm.

Andrew grunts and sips his gin

Andrew Anyhow—let's hope he's got some good news for us.

Jane What about?

Andrew Oh, I just thought perhaps he might have got that job in West
  Hartlepool.
Jane Good heavens. I'd forgotten all about that.
Andrew *I* hadn't.
Jane Sally wouldn't see so much of him then.

Andrew pretends he had not thought of that

Andrew Oh, dear. That would be a shame.
Jane (*with an amused smile*) You've never really liked Geoff very much,
  have you?
Andrew Well, I . . . Haven't I? I can't think how she got to know him in
  the first place.
Jane You know perfectly well. He was a pen-friend.
Andrew A pen-friend? He comes from Stoke Poges.
Jane What's that got to do with it?
Andrew Other men's daughters have pen-friends in Biarritz or Bermuda.
  Mine has to pick one from Stokes Poges.
Jane Sally always was bad at geography.
Andrew Sorry?
Jane She thought that Stoke Poges was in the Seychelles.
Andrew Anyhow, if he's a pen-friend what's he doing spending weekends
  with us? Pen-friends are supposed to write to you, not stay with you.
Jane It's nice for him to relax on a Saturday and Sunday.
Andrew Why does he have to do it in *my* house?
Jane He works hard all the week.
Andrew Oh, does he? I didn't know he worked at all. What does he do?
Jane He's training to be a gardener.
Andrew Going to spend all his time planting cabbages?
Jane And he's looking for a house in London.
Andrew He'll have to plant a few cabbages to pay for that!
Jane Don't be silly, darling. They'll be sharing it with four others.
Andrew Four other cabbages?
Jane No, you idiot! Four other people.
Andrew Oh, I see. A commune.
Jane It's the *in* thing these days.
Andrew Does that mean that Sally's going to go and live with him?
Jane Wouldn't be surprised.
Andrew Good lord . . .
Jane He'll probably mention it to you one of these days during dinner.
Andrew I sincerely hope he doesn't. Otherwise *I'll* be the one choking on
  the avocado!

She laughs and hits him affectionately with the newspaper

*Geoff appears in the garden. He is a good-looking young man, carrying a
week-end grip*

*Andrew and Jane do not notice him. He sees the ladder leaning against the
wall and looks puzzled. He goes nearer to it and looks up at the top of it*

Want another drink?

Jane Not for me, thanks. I must go and see about the dinner.

Andrew (*rising*) Well, I think I'll just top mine up a bit.

Outside Geoff glances around to make sure he is alone and then puts down his bag and begins to go up the ladder. Inside, Jane sees him and reacts slowly, peering with disbelief into the garden

Jane Good heavens . . . There's a man outside climbing up our ladder.

Andrew (*hopefully*) Aah! Perhaps your window cleaner's turned up, after all.

Jane No! It's Geoff!

Andrew (*without enthusiasm*) Oh, God! (*He pours a larger drink*)

Jane goes quickly out into the garden. Andrew follows with his gin. They peer up at the slowly climbing figure

Jane (*eventually*) Geoff!

Geoff reacts and nearly falls

What on earth are you doing up there?

Geoff (*smiling feebly*) Oh, hullo. I say, it's a lovely view of the garden!

Andrew and Jane exchange a look

Jane Yes, it is, isn't it?

Geoff (*enthusiastically*) You can see it all from up here, you know. Phlox, and hollyhocks, and those nice yellow daisy things with red middles.

Andrew Gaillardias.

Geoff Is that what they're called?

Andrew (*moving to Jane*) Thought he was training to be a gardener. Yellow daisy things with red middles . . .

Geoff You know, I've never been up a ladder before! (*He beams with joy as he surveys the garden*)

Jane (*anxiously*) Well, do hold on, Geoff. We don't want you to go and fall. Do we, Andrew?

Andrew What?

She gives him a look

Oh, no. No, we don't want that.

Geoff (*enthusiastically*) You know, I rather like being up a ladder!

Andrew You should join the Fire Brigade.

Jane (*anxiously*) I do think you ought to come down now, Geoff. I mean —it is rather dangerous up there and accidents do happen.

Andrew They certainly do. Especially in this house.

Geoff Oh—all right, then. (*He slips and nearly falls*) Oooh!

Jane (*alarmed*) Are you all right?

Geoff Yes. I think so. Here I come. (*He starts to come down the ladder*)

Jane Now remember—one step at a time.

Andrew Rungs, darling.

Jane What?
Andrew One rung at a time.
Jane Oh, yes. Rungs.

Geoff arrives safely on terra firma, exhilarated by his experience

Geoff It's wonderful up there! Beautiful view. You should try it sometime.
Andrew She did.
Geoff What?
Andrew Yes. Up the ladder.
Geoff (*to Jane*) *You* went up the ladder?
Jane Well, I'd given up the window-cleaner.
Geoff Oh? Is this *his* ladder?
Andrew No, no. It's *our* ladder. We've got a ladder, you see, but no window-cleaner. Very aggravating. Well! You got down for the week-end again, then?
Geoff (*nervously*) Yes, rather! As a matter of fact I—er—I specially wanted to be here this week-end. Got something to talk to you about.
Andrew Got some news for us?
Geoff Yes.
Andrew *Good* news?
Geoff I hope so.
Andrew (*smiling*) You're going to West Hartlepool?
Geoff (*puzzled*) What?
Andrew (*his face falling*) You're *not* going to West Hartlepool?
Geoff Well, it wasn't that exactly.
Andrew Nothing to do with West Hartlepool?
Geoff No.
Andrew What a pity. (*He sits on the garden chair*)
Geoff It—it wasn't about work, as a matter of fact.
Andrew Oh. About something else, was it?

Geoff smiles nervously

Geoff Yes. I've found a house!
Jane (*delightedly*) Geoff!
Geoff With some friends of mine.
Jane Oh, that *is* exciting! (*She sits on the garden seat*) Did you hear that, Andrew? Geoff's found a house with some friends of his. Isn't that wonderful?
Andrew Wonderful. Now I suppose the price of cabbages will go up.
Geoff What?
Andrew Nothing.
Geoff (*gaining confidence*) Of course, there's a lot to be done. Some of the walls are collapsing a bit. They'll have to be made good. Well—*you* know how it is.
Andrew Do we? (*He exchanges a look with Jane*)
Geoff And then the plumbing leaves a bit to be desired, but Peter's good with pipes so that's all right. Then, of course, the whole place needs to be redecorated.

Andrew Well that should keep you busy at the week-ends.

Jane gives him a stern look

Jane That really *is* good news, Geoff. I'm so glad.
Andrew Was that what you wanted to tell us?

Geoff loses confidence again

Geoff Well—no, . . . not *just* that.

Andrew rises ominously

Andrew Something else, was it?
Geoff Yes.
Andrew Well? (*Pause*) Well, what was it? (*Pause*) You haven't forgotten already, have you?
Geoff Oh, no! No. I was just. . . .
Jane Plucking up courage?
Geoff Yes.

Andrew looks at him suspiciously

Andrew Needs plucking up, does it?
Geoff Well—just a little, yes. A couple of notches. It's—it's about Sally.
Andrew (*heavily*) About Sally, is it?
Geoff (*nodding nervously*) Yes.
Andrew I see. (*Moving to Jane*) We're not having avocados tonight, are we?

Jane giggles. Andrew sits beside her. Geoff looks puzzled

Geoff Sorry?
Andrew (*to Geoff*) Just a little in-joke with my wife.
Geoff Oh . . .
Jane (*tactfully*) Well, I think I'll leave you two men alone to talk about things . . . (*She starts to go*)
Andrew Oh, no, you won't! (*He catches her arm and pulls her back again*) If he's got something to say to me about Sally he can wait till after dinner. I'd rather face it on a full stomach.
Geoff Oh, well, in that case *I'll* go. (*He starts to go*)
Andrew (*hopefully*) For good?

Geoff stops and turns

Geoff Upstairs.
Andrew Ah.
Geoff To freshen up.
Andrew Good idea. You know which room you're in, don't you?
Geoff Yes, thanks.
Andrew You should do by now.
Jane (*quietly*) Andrew . . .!

Geoff Right. I'll see you both later on, then.
Andrew More than likely, yes.
Jane And Geoff—congratulations!
Geoff What?
Jane About the house.
Geoff Oh, that. Yes. Right. Thanks.

*Geoff, smiling nervously, stumbles off into the house and out into the hall
Jane crosses behind the seat, watching Geoff go*

Jane Really, Andrew! You didn't make it very easy for him.
Andrew Why should I? If Sally's going to live with him and Peter and
three or four other people in a collapsing house with no plumbing I
intend to make things as difficult as possible for him.
Jane But he's such a nice young man. If he worked at your bank you'd be
delighted.
Andrew I'd be surprised.

Jane is about to leave, but remembers something

Jane By the way—you'll never guess who rang today.
Andrew Really?
Jane Well—go on.
Andrew What?
Jane Guess.
Andrew You just said I'd never guess.
Jane Well try.
Andrew I haven't the remotest idea.
Jane The Vicar.
Andrew You were right. I'd never have guessed. You mean the . . .? (*He
mimes a clerical collar and puts his hands together in prayer*)
Jane Yes.
Andrew Vicar?
Jane Yes. He wants to come to tea.
Andrew *Here?*
Jane Yes.
Andrew Good heavens. What on earth does he want to come to tea *here*
for?
Jane He's new to the village.
Andrew That's no excuse.
Jane Oh, Andrew . . .! (*She laughs reprovingly*)

*Inside, Geoff appears from the hall, having left his week-end grip in the
garden. He heads for the garden but pauses to look at something that
catches his eye in the newspaper*

Jane I expect he's visiting all his parishioners. Trying to get to know
them. I expect he's keen.
Andrew Oh, is he? We'll soon put a stop to that.

Andrew rises, puts his glass down and drifts thoughtfully across the garden

Jane (*a sudden thought*) Good heavens . . .!
Andrew What?
Jane You don't suppose he heard that the window-cleaner came here and
  didn't get away alive?

*Inside, Geoff looks up from the newspaper, somewhat surprised by the re-
mark he has just overheard*

Andrew I sincerely hope not.
Jane (*moving closer to Andrew*) Perhaps that's what he wants to talk to
  us about.
Andrew About the window-cleaner?
Jane Yes.
Andrew Now, wait a minute. If he *had* heard about what happened to the
  window-cleaner he wouldn't want to come here himself, would he?
Jane Too risky, you mean?
Andrew Well, yes, of course. (*He sits thoughtfully on the garden chair*)
  Mind you. Let's be fair. We've never had a vicar done to death here
  before, have we?

*Geoff now looks distinctly alarmed. He edges nearer to the garden door,
listening intently*

Jane No, and I certainly hope we're not going to start now.
Andrew You can't be sure. Ask a vicar to tea—*any*thing could happen.
  H'm. A bit too risky, I'd say . . .
Jane For him?
Andrew No, no—for *us!* With our luck we'd never get away with it.

*Geoff's alarm is increasing. He cannot believe his ears. He peers nervously
out of the door into the garden*

Jane Does seem a shame, though. He was awfully keen to come. I think
  we *will* have to do it some time, Andrew.

*A pause. Andrew thinks for a moment, then makes a decision and slaps his
knee decisively*

Andrew All right. Let's do it! Get it over with. And if the worst comes to
  the worst we must be quite sure that nobody finds out. They're very
  fond of vicars in this village, and if he came here and kicked the bucket
  they'd never let us hear the last of it.
Jane We'll just have to be very careful, that's all, darling. I'll give him a
  ring in the morning and ask him to tea. (*She looks at her watch*) Good
  heavens! I'd better go and see about dinner.

*Jane runs into the house, passing Geoff on her way. He is pale and still.
Andrew returns to the seat—and his gin*

  (*Cheerfully*) Hullo, Geoff! Have a good wash? (*She disappears into the
  hall*)

Geoff looks apprehensively at Andrew. Andrew settles himself comfortably

*on the garden seat, enjoying the pleasant evening sunshine. Geoff hovers
nervously*

Geoff Oh. Sorry.
Andrew H'm?
Geoff I left my. . . .

Andrew looks up

Andrew What?
Geoff Things.
Andrew Oh. Yes.

Andrew leans back and closes his eyes. Geoff goes to collect his bag

Have a good wash?
Geoff Er—not yet. (*He returns to the garden seat with his bag*)
Andrew Never mind. Plenty of time. We shan't be eating for ages. Perhaps
you'd like a drink? You look as if you could do with one.
Geoff I—I don't.

Andrew opens his eyes

Andrew What?
Geoff Drink.
Andrew Good lord . . .
Geoff Apple juice.
Andrew What?
Geoff That's what I drink. Apple juice.
Andrew I don't think we've got any of that. (*He closes his eyes again*)

Geoff hovers. He puts down his bag and goes to Andrew again

Geoff I've got a confession to make.
Andrew Yes, I know. You've found a house.
Geoff No, no. Not that. (*Emphatically*) I didn't have my wash!
Andrew Nothing to get excited about.
Geoff I came downstairs to get my things—but I didn't come straight out
here!

*Andrew looks at him for a moment, unable to understand Geoff's vehemence
over such trivia*

Andrew Is this important?
Geoff (*strongly*) I stood for some time in the sitting-room!
Andrew You needn't have done that. There are plenty of chairs in there.
Geoff The point is—I heard what you were saying about the Vicar!

No reaction from Andrew. He is enjoying the warmth of the sunshine

Andrew Oh, that. Yes. (*He chuckles*) He wants to come to tea.
Geoff (*anxiously*) Are you going to let him?
Andrew Probably. Yes. After all, he's new to the parish.
Geoff You're not really going to *do* it, though, are you?

Andrew (*dreamily*) Do what?
Geoff Kill the Vicar off!
Andrew Well, that rather depends.
Geoff Depends on what?
Andrew On whether he's a lucky vicar or an unlucky vicar.
Geoff And if he's *un*lucky?
Andrew Too bad.
Geoff Oh, my God! (*He moves away, appalled*)
Andrew (*wearily*) Did you *have* to listen in to all that? *I* don't like it any more than *you* do . . . (*He sips his gin wretchedly*) And anyhow—he did invite himself. We didn't invite him.
Geoff Well, you'll have to put him off!

Jane enters from the hall and heads for the garden

Andrew You know, it's a pity you spent so long standing in the sitting-room. You would never have known about this. (*Kindly*) Look, Geoff —you needn't worry. It may never happen.
Geoff But if it does?
Andrew (*confidently*) Well, I expect the Curate's quite capable of managing on his own.

Geoff sinks in despair on to the garden chair. Jane comes out into the garden

Jane Leeks out of the garden! Isn't that exciting? (*She sees Geoff's face*) Geoff, are you all right?
Andrew He's been skulking in the sitting-room listening to our conversation.
Jane Which part?
Andrew The part about the Vicar.
Jane Oh, really, Geoff! You shouldn't have listened. That was a private conversation. Anyway, I wouldn't worry about it. It may never happen.
Geoff (*desperately*) But you're asking him to tea!
Jane (*reasonably*) Well, it was his *idea*.

Geoff rises in a state of great agitation

Geoff Then you'll have to put him off!
Jane Oh, I don't think I can do that. It would be awfully rude. (*She sits beside Andrew on the garden seat*)
Geoff You don't seem to understand—I heard what you said! You're going to kill him!
Andrew (*beginning to get rattled*) Look, you can't blame *us* if something happens to the Vicar.
Jane And *you're* the one who doesn't seem to understand—
Geoff He's going to die right here in this house!
Andrew Not necessarily. It doesn't happen to *everyone* who comes to visit, you know. Otherwise, it would be impossible to get a four for bridge.

Andrew and Jane are amused by this. Geoff is not

Geoff Oh, my God! (*He turns away from them*)

Andrew and Jane exchange a look, then Andrew turns again to Geoff

Andrew Now, look here—whenever this sort of thing happens, it's deeply embarrassing for us. I hope you realize that.

Geoff looks at him with fearful apprehension

Geoff You—you don't mean—you don't mean that this sort of thing—has happened *before*?

Andrew looks at Jane. She gives a helpless shrug. He turns back to Geoff

Andrew (*with a great effort*) Well—yes, as a matter of fact. I'm afraid it has.

A pause. Geoff is frozen

Geoff Often?
Andrew Fairly often.
Geoff *How* often?
Andrew Well, if you must know—(*with difficulty*)—six times.
Geoff (*appalled*) *Six!*
Andrew I'm afraid so. (*He rises with his empty glass to above the garden seat*) Now you can see why we don't want people to know about it, can't you?
Geoff Yes, I certainly can!
Jane We've even thought of moving away from here.
Geoff (*suspiciously*) To get away from it all?
Andrew Yes. We thought perhaps we ought to go to another house. Start all over again.
Geoff What?!
Andrew In the hope that perhaps next time we'll be a little luckier.
Geoff (*wildly*) You seem to have been pretty lucky up to now!
Andrew What do you mean?
Geoff Well—after all—nothing's happened to *you*, has it? I mean, you've never been to prison, have you?
Andrew (*puzzled*) To prison?
Geoff Yes! To prison!

Andrew and Jane look bewildered

Andrew Er—no. Should I have?
Geoff (*heavily*) Well, *some* people might think so!

A pause

Andrew (*to Jane*) I think I need some more gin. How about you? (*He goes towards the house*)
Jane No, thanks. I really must get on with the dinner. You mustn't worry about it, you know, Geoff. It could happen to anyone. (*She follows Andrew inside*)
Andrew Funny chap . . .

Jane H'm?

Andrew What's all this about me being a prison visitor?

Jane Perhaps he thought you looked the type.

Andrew Extraordinary. (*He starts to pour himself a drink*)

Geoff comes in quickly from the garden

Geoff Who *were* they?

Andrew Who?

Geoff The six!

Jane Do you really want to know?

Geoff Yes! I do!

Jane looks at Andrew resignedly

Andrew (*with difficulty*) Oh—er—well—let's see now. There was the little man who read the gas meter. What was his name, darling?

Jane Mr Merry.

Andrew (*amused in spite of everything*) Was it really?

Jane Yes. Percy Merry.

Andrew Percy Merry! Good lord . . . (*He chuckles*)

Geoff What happened to him?

Andrew Ah—well, you see—the gas meter's in the cellar here. Down a long flight of stone steps. (*He sits on the sofa*)

Jane I warned him they were rather steep three or four times, but he never seemed to pay any attention.

Andrew Then one day—they must have been very slippery or something.

Geoff (*fearfully*) And Mr Merry?

Andrew Wasn't merry any more.

Geoff He—fell?

Andrew Apparently. Must have gone down that flight of steps like a bob-sleigh champion.

Geoff So what did they do about it?

Andrew Who?

Geoff The authorities!

Andrew Nothing very much. We've had our gas bills estimated ever since.

Jane perches on the arm of the sofa

Jane Then there was the window-cleaner . . .

Geoff (*wildly*) Fell off his ladder, I suppose?

Andrew How did *you* know?

Geoff I guessed!

Jane Some of the steps were wonky.

Andrew Rungs, darling.

Jane What?

Andrew Rungs in ladders. Steps in stairs.

Jane Oh, yes.

Geoff moves wildly round to Andrew

Geoff And nobody came to see you about it? To ask you questions?

Andrew Very little point, really. He was dead all right.

Geoff Oh, my God! I need a drink. (*He subsides into the armchair*)

Andrew (*to Jane*) Got any apple juice?

Geoff Something stronger!

Andrew I'll get you a whisky. (*He goes to get a whisky*)

Geoff I just can't believe it. Six already and the Vicar on the way! If you go on like this you'll soon be into double figures. (*He looks at Jane*) You're taking this very calmly.

Jane Well, there's nothing else we can do. We don't seem to be able to stop it.

Andrew (*arriving with the whisky*) Whisky!

Geoff Thanks.

Andrew Better than apple juice. (*He chuckles, looking at Geoff*)

Geoff takes the glass and is about to drink it, but hesitates and looks at Andrew suspiciously

Something wrong?

Geoff I'm not sure . . .

Andrew takes the glass, sniffs at it, starts to hand it back to Geoff but changes his mind, takes a sip and hands it back

Andrew Very good.

Reassured, Geoff downs the whisky in one

I thought you weren't used to whisky.

Geoff It's dreadful . . .!

Andrew It shouldn't be at that price!

Geoff No, no! Not the drink! The—the *other* business . . .

Andrew Oh, that. Yes. Yes, I suppose it is, isn't it? (*Moving to the window seat*) All the same, I think you should try to be a bit more sympathetic. After all, it isn't *our* fault.

Geoff Then whose fault is it?

Jane (*reasonably*) It isn't anybody's fault, Geoff. I suppose it's just— well, I dunno—something about this house.

But Geoff is sunk in gloom, a long way from reassurance

Sally comes in from the hall, having arrived home from work. She is a pretty, vivacious girl of about twenty

Andrew Oh, hullo darling. (*They kiss briefly*)

Sally I say, Daddy—did you know there's a ladder leaning against the side of the house?

Andrew Yes. We're trying to tempt a passing window cleaner. Had a hard day behind your typewriter?

Sally Yes. I'm exhausted. Mr Gledhill always starts dictating letters at twenty-five past five. I could kill him.

Andrew Don't do that! We have enough problems.

Sally looks across at Geoff

Sally Hullo, you!

Geoff does not react

Is he asleep?
Andrew No. Thinking.
Sally Geoff. . . .

Still no reaction. Sally goes to Jane and kisses her briefly

Hullo, Mummy.
Jane Hullo, darling.
Sally I had lunch with Hilary today.
Jane Oh, good. I haven't seen her for ages. Is she still mad about riding?
Sally H'm. I might pop over to their place sometime tomorrow. They've got a new horse.
Andrew I didn't know they'd eaten the last one yet.

Sally looks at him pityingly. Andrew looks a little shamefaced

Sally Daddy, that really is one of your worst.
Andrew Yes, I know. I'm sorry.
Sally (*to Jane*) I don't know how you live with this man.
Jane I've got no choice. He owns the house.

Sally looks at Geoff again

Sally Is he all right?
Andrew Bit moody.
Sally You haven't said anything to upset him, have you? (*She goes across to Geoff*)

Andrew and Jane exchange a furtive glance

Geoff!

Geoff comes to at last

Geoff Oh! Hullo, Sal . . .
Sally You were miles away.
Geoff (*miserably*) I wish I was!
Sally What?
Geoff I mean yes, I was. I was dreaming.
Sally (*seeing his glass*) Have you been drinking?
Geoff (*miles away*) No. I've got one, thanks.
Sally It's empty.
Geoff (*coming to*) Oh—yes, so it is.
Sally Would you like another?
Geoff Definitely!

Sally looks surprised

Andrew (*taking the glass*) I'll do that. (*He goes to see to the drink*)
Geoff (*alarmed*) No! Don't *you* bother!
Sally (*surprised*) He *can* manage to pour a drink, you know. He's had plenty of practice. (*She grins at Andrew*)

Andrew (*to Sally*) Sherry for you?
Sally Yes, please.

Andrew sees to the drinks

(*To Geoff*) Would you like to go out into the garden?
Geoff (*nervously*) Why? What's happened?

Sally smiles at Geoff patiently

Sally Nothing's happened. It's just a lovely evening, that's all. I thought
we could have our drinks out there. It's so romantic.

*But Geoff looks far from romantic. Sally looks at Jane and shrugs. Andrew
arrives with a sherry for Sally and a whisky for Geoff*

Andrew (*to Sally*) Right then, here's yours.
Sally Thanks, Daddy. (*She takes it*)
Andrew (*to Geoff*) And here's *yours*. . . .

*Geoff takes the whisky and is about to drink some of it when Andrew starts
to chuckle. Geoff stops, his drink poised, and looks at Andrew*

It's not out of the same decanter.
Geoff (*apprehensively*) Oh, my God . . .!

*Geoff abruptly holds out the whisky to Andrew. Andrew smiles happily, and
takes the glass. He takes a sip of it and, acting as if poisoned, falls back
on to the sofa and beats it with one hand. Jane and Sally watch with amuse-
ment. Finally, Andrew gets to his feet with a grin and hands the drink back
to the embarrassed Geoff*

(*Abruptly*) Thanks.
Andrew Don't mention it. I always wanted to be a whisky taster. (*He
moves away to Jane with a grin and sits on the sofa*)

Sally turns to Geoff

Sally Whisky? Are you drinking whisky? You don't usually.
Geoff I'm trying to calm my nerves.
Sally What are you nervous about?
Andrew All that money he's going to lay out, I should think.
Sally What money?
Jane Haven't you heard the news? Hasn't he told you the news?
Sally Has he *got* some news?
Andrew Yes. He certainly has.
Sally He's not going to West Hartlepool, is he?
Andrew No. I'm afraid not.
Jane He's found a house.
Sally (*delightedly*) He *hasn't*!
Jane Yes, he has.
Sally A house?
Andrew Yes. And when the walls are built and the pipes are laid, it's
going to sleep about forty-seven.

Sally A *house?*
Andrew Well, they had to call it *something.*

Sally turns excitedly to Geoff

Sally You've found a house! (*Geoff is too deep in gloom to reply*) He's found a house!
Andrew Don't *keep* saying it.
Jane Isn't it wonderful?
Sally Terrific! (*To Geoff*) Why are you looking so miserable when you've found a house?
Geoff I'll be all right in a minute.
Sally I hope so. Come on! (*She pulls Geoff to his feet*) Let's go into the garden!
Geoff Oh. All right. If you want to.

Sally leads him towards the garden

Sally Give us a shout if you want some help, Mummy.
Jane All right.

Sally and Geoff go out into the garden and sit side-by-side on the seat

They're such a sweet couple.
Andrew (*without enthusiasm*) Huh.

Jane gives him a gently reproving smile and gets up

Jane Come on. You can talk to me while I peel the potatoes.

Jane goes out into the hall

Andrew hangs back to look out of the window

Andrew You'd think that boy would be more sympathetic. Typical of his generation. Think of no-one but themselves . . .

Andrew goes out into the hall with his drink as the dialogue starts out in the garden

Sally Why didn't you phone me at the office and tell me?
Geoff Tell you what?
Sally About finding a house! You clever old thing. (*She kisses him enthusiastically*)
Geoff Oh, that . . .
Sally So did you talk to my father?
Geoff (*ruefully*) Oh, yes. We talked all right!
Sally And what did he say?
Geoff (*miles away*) H'm?
Sally About us! Moving in with Peter and the others.
Geoff (*miserably*) Poor Percy . . .

Sally looks puzzled

Sally I thought his name was Peter.
Geoff What?
Sally Michael's friend.

Geoff looks blank

The other chap who's going to share the house with us. (*She waves a hand in front of his blank eyes*) Geoff! The one who's good at plumbing!

He rises agitatedly away from her

Geoff I wasn't talking about him. I was talking about Percy.
Sally Percy? Percy who?
Geoff Merry.
Sally *Who?*

He turns and looks at her in astonishment

Geoff You've never heard of Percy Merry?
Sally No.
Geoff You never *met* him?
Sally (*puzzled*) No.

He paces away below her like a caged lion

Geoff Well, you won't *now*! He used to come in and out of here quite often.
Sally Who did?
Geoff Percy Merry. To read the meter.

Sally looks blank

The gas meter. (*Secretively*) And you know where that is, don't you? (*He points downwards knowingly*)
Sally Well, of course I know where the gas meter is! I just didn't know that a Mr Merry came to read it.
Geoff Well, he won't any more. (*He returns urgently and sits beside her again*) Here! What about his wife?
Sally (*uninterestedly*) Well, *she* can read it if if she wants to.
Geoff Didn't you even send her a bunch of flowers?
Sally What?
Geoff Lilies. Something like that. Afterwards.

Sally does not know what he is talking about

Sally Why should I send lilies to a perfect stranger?
Geoff (*loudly*) And what about the window-cleaner?
Sally I didn't send *him* flowers, either.
Geoff You could have sent them to his wife, though.
Sally How ever many whiskies has Daddy given you?
Geoff Only two. I shall need a hell of a lot more than that to forget what I've heard tonight!
Sally Geoff—what *are* you talking about?
Geoff I'm talking about people! People who—died—*here*. Six of them!

Sally looks puzzled

Sally Six?

He nods solemnly

Geoff Six.

Sally I thought it was only four.

Geoff No—six. Definitely six. There was Mr Merry and the window-cleaner and . . . (*He breaks off*) What do you mean you thought it was only four?

Sally (*thinking hard*) They can't have told me about two of them. Are you sure it was six?

Geoff looks glazed

Geoff That's what they said.

Sally (*realizing*) Ah—yes, of *course*—I didn't know about Mr Merry and the window-cleaner, did I? Yes, that *would* make six.

Geoff You—you mean—you mean you've known all along about the "others"? Ever since we met?

Sally (*blithely*) Oh, yes.

Geoff And you didn't think to—well, to sort of—mention it?

Sally Well, I didn't want you to know. We like to keep it quiet. I mean, we don't want people talking about it or we'll have no friends left.

Geoff cannot believe her calm acceptance of the situation

Geoff But aren't you even shocked?

Sally Come off it, Geoff! It's not *our* fault, is it? These things happen. It's just unfortunate. It doesn't make any difference to *us*, surely?

She tries to cuddle up to him but he is not in the mood to co-operate

Geoff Well, I—I did think it made a little bit of a difference, yes!

Sally gets a bit cross

Sally You're not even sympathetic, are you?

Geoff Sympathetic?

Sally Well, it's not very nice for us, either, you know!

Sally turns away from him, angry at his attitude. Geoff is surprised to find himself under attack and subsides into silence

> *Inside, Andrew comes in quickly from the hall, goes to the drinks table and picks up the bottle of gin. He is obviously anxious to hide it somewhere*

Sarah (*off*) Andrew!

> *Before Andrew can hide the bottle, Sarah comes in from the hall. She is Andrew's sister, a good-looking woman of about fifty, well-dressed but inclined to be forgetful. Andrew conceals the gin behind his back*

Andrew! Why are you running away?

Andrew I wasn't running away.

Sarah Yes, you were. You saw me coming downstairs and you ran away. That's not a very nice way to treat your sister. (*She looks at him suspiciously*) What have you got behind your back?

Andrew (*guiltily*) W-what?

Sarah You're hiding something.

Andrew No, I'm not.

Sarah Yes, you are! Andrew. . . .!

He tries to elude her, but she dodges around him and sees the bottle of gin

Andrew—it's a bottle of gin.

Andrew What? (*He looks at the gin as if seeing it for the first time*) Good lord. So it is.

Sarah What were you doing with a bottle of gin behind your back?

Andrew I was hiding it. I mean I was looking for it! (*He chuckles*) And here it is. So that's all right, isn't it?

Sarah You weren't trying to hide it from *me*, were you?

Andrew (*innocently*) What a suggestion. Of course not, Sarah.

Sarah You're being very furtive. Had you forgotten I was coming for the weekend?

Andrew How could I forget a thing like that? I bought this bottle of gin specially. Does Jane know you're here?

Sarah (*vaguely*) Who?

Andrew Jane. The woman I'm married to.

Sarah Oh, *that* Jane! Of course she knows. I arrived this afternoon before she went shopping. Didn't she tell you?

Andrew No. Don't suppose she thought it was important.

Sarah What?

Andrew Well—you know what I mean.

Sarah (*smiling contentedly*) I had a bath and fell asleep.

Andrew Did you really? Good lord. Well, now you're awake and you've found the gin so you're all right, aren't you?

Sarah There's no need to make me sound like an alcoholic. I have been seen *without* a glass in my hand.

Andrew Not after six in the evening you haven't! Tonic?

Sarah Just a little. (*She sits on the sofa*) Do you know it's over six weeks since I saw you?

Andrew Is it really? Well, I don't suppose I've changed very much in that time.

Outside, Geoff notices the new arrival through the window

Geoff Sal . . .?

Sally (*abruptly*) What?

Geoff Are you expecting anyone *else* for dinner?

Sally No. I don't think so. Why?

Inside, Andrew comes down to the sofa, heading for Sarah with her drink. Geoff sees Andrew, a big smile on his face, approaching an apparently strange lady with a drink containing God knows what. So he panics, and before Sally can stop him he rushes into the house. Sally follows in puzzled surprise

Where are you going?

Inside, Sarah takes the drink from Andrew and looks astonished as a distraught young man rushes in from the garden

Geoff Stop!!

Sarah and Andrew look at him in surprise. He comes to Sarah and points to the drink in her hand

What's that?
Sarah Er—I beg your pardon?
Geoff That! *That!* What is it?
Sarah Well, it's—(*she looks at the drink*)—it's a small gin—(*she looks reprovingly at Andrew*)—and *far* too much tonic, Andrew!
Andrew Oh, dear. Have I drowned it?
Sarah It would need to be very strong to survive in that lot.

Andrew goes back to the drinks table

Geoff Are you sure?
Sarah What?
Geoff That that's *all* it is!
Sarah Andrew doesn't usually make mistakes with his drinks. (*She prepares to drink*)
Geoff No!
Sarah (*astonished*) What?
Geoff Give it to me!

Geoff takes the drink from her abruptly. Sarah rises in astonishment, unable to believe her eyes

Sarah Just a minute! What on earth . . . ?
Sally Geoff, what *are* you doing?

Geoff moves quickly round below the sofa to Andrew, with Sally following him. He holds the drink out to Andrew

Geoff *You* try it!

Andrew gives a patient smile. He takes the drink, tastes a little and hands it back to Geoff. Sarah and Sally watch in astonishment

Andrew Tastes perfectly all right to me.

Geoff is a little taken aback

Geoff Oh. Good. That's all right then. (*He goes back to Sarah and gives her the drink with an embarrassed smile*) There you are. It's all right.
Sarah Thank you. (*She takes the drink and looks at Geoff, totally bemused*) Are you in the habit of bursting into strange houses and taking people's drinks away from them?

Sally comes to the rescue

Sally Aunt Sarah—this is Geoff.
Sarah Oh! So *you're* Geoff! (*Knowingly*) I've heard all about *you*. I

suppose you've come down for the week-end again. (*She looks out of the window*)

Geoff Aunt Sarah? (*He hisses nervously at Sally*) Why didn't you *say* so? I thought he was giving a drink to a strange woman.

Sally What difference would that make? Honestly, I don't know what's got into you today. (*She sits, disgruntled, in the armchair*)

Andrew, having got himself a drink, wanders towards Sarah

Andrew You any good at brick-laying, Sarah?

Sarah turns from the window in surprise

Sarah Brick-laying? Why?

Andrew He's just found a house and some of his walls need a little encouragement.

Sarah (*confidentially*) You'd think he'd be *pleased* to have found a house, wouldn't you?

Andrew (*thoughtfully*) Yes. I suppose you would really . . .

Sarah He doesn't *look* very pleased, though, does he?

Andrew Very difficult to tell with a face like that.

Andrew turns and bumps into Geoff. Geoff reacts away and sits nervously on the sofa

Sally So it's six now, then, Daddy?

Andrew Oh—he told you, did he?

Sally Yes. Did you *have* to tell him? I didn't want him to know.

Andrew He wouldn't have known if he hadn't left his bag out there in the garden.

Sarah crosses to Geoff

Sarah Ah! So they've told you all about Mr Merry and the others, then?

Geoff Yes, they certainly have!

Sarah sits beside Geoff on the sofa

Sarah Isn't it unfortunate?

Geoff gazes at her incredulously

Geoff Is *that* what you call it? Unfortunate?

Sarah (*confidentially*) Now look, you won't go gossiping and spreading it around, will you? We don't want *every*one to know about it.

Geoff No, I bet you don't!

Sarah It'd be such a shame if they had to go and live somewhere else. They're so very fond of this place.

Geoff Even after what's happened here?

Sarah (*sighing fatalistically*) Well, they've just been unlucky, you see.

Geoff can only stare at her in disbelief

Jane comes in from the hall

Jane Dinner won't be very long.

Sarah Good. I'm starving!

Geoff (*to Sarah, urgently*) How can you take it so calmly?
Sarah Well, I *have* had dinner here before.
Geoff No, no! I mean—why aren't you down at the church?
Sarah It's Friday evening. I never pray on a Friday evening.
Geoff Warning the Vicar!
Sarah What?
Geoff He's coming here to tea!
Sarah Oh, good! (*She looks delightedly at Andrew*) I thought it was time you got around to *him*, Andrew.
Andrew Oh, we didn't invite him. He invited himself.
Jane He's new here, you see.
Geoff (*to Sarah*) Aren't you going to stop him?
Sarah What?
Geoff Coming to tea!
Sarah Why should I do that? After all, they are his parishioners.
Jane (*brightly*) I do hope everyone likes leeks. They're out of the garden. (*She smiles sweetly at Sally*)
Geoff (*to Sarah, desperately*) Aren't you going to warn him? Aren't you going to tell somebody?
Andrew Will you stop firing questions at my sister? She's trying to enjoy her aperitif, before she has her leeks.
Sally Geoff, what *is* the matter with you? I don't see why *you're* upset. It's much worse for us than it is for you.
Geoff I think I'm going to be sick . . .
Andrew Oh, that's charming. I like that. The minute I introduce you to my sister you start to feel sick. (*To Sarah*) Come along, Sarah. Let's take our drinks into the garden. (*He pulls Sarah to her feet*)
Sarah What a good idea. You coming, Jane?
Jane I think so. For a few minutes.

Andrew leads Sarah and Jane out into the garden

Sarah (*as they go*) It's the best time of the day, isn't it? You can smell the honeysuckle. Your garden really is looking lovely at the moment.
Jane Yes, it is, isn't it? I was looking at it from the top of the ladder at tea-time.
Sarah Good heavens! Wasn't that rather dangerous?
Jane Oh, don't worry. I held on tight.

Andrew, Jane and Sarah laugh and disappear down the garden. Occasionally a ripple of laughter can be heard from them during the scene that now follows inside

Rather fed-up, Sally gets up and goes towards the window

Sally I don't know what's got into you this evening. There was no need to over-react like that. You gave poor Aunt Sarah the fright of her life.
Geoff Well, I didn't know who she was, did I? I've never met her before. I was only trying to protect her.
Sally Protect her? From what?

Geoff (*with difficulty*) Well—after what your father told me, I couldn't be sure *what* was going to happen to her, could I?

Sally Not a lot could happen to her sitting down!

Geoff I wouldn't be too sure about that!

Sally (*edgily*) Well! This is going to be a really great weekend with you in this mood! (*She turns away and looks out of the window*)

Geoff Look—be reasonable! I didn't know about Percy Merry and all that lot before. It's bound to make a difference.

Sally (*turning*) I don't see why. After all, it's nothing for *you* to be upset about. (*Returning to him*) How do you think Mummy and Daddy feel? It can't be very nice for them, wondering if dinner guests are going to pass out before the pudding! (*She sits beside him and cuddles up close*) Oh, come on Geoff—don't let's think about that. Let's think about *this*. (*She cuddles up to him sexily*)

Geoff (*miserably*) But that's just the trouble! Now I know about *that*, I can't concentrate on *this*. I mean—how long will it be before the next one?

Sally How do *I* know? But it's months now since the last one so maybe our luck's changing.

Geoff (*wildly*) Oh, don't lose heart! The Vicar's coming to tea next week!

Sally (*patiently*) Don't be silly, darling. Nothing'll happen to the Vicar.

Geoff Don't you be too sure!

Sally (*close to him*) No, no. The window-cleaner was the last one. I'm certain of it. I just have the feeling that we're going to be luckier from now on. You see.

Geoff But I . . .

She stops his mouth with a kiss. He surfaces and attempts to continue speaking

I heard what they . . .

She kisses him again

Sally Dinner will be ready soon. I must go and change.

Before he can protest any further Sally runs off into the hall

There is a burst of laughter out in the garden. Geoff is left, still troubled. He goes to the drinks table to pour himself a large whisky. He tries the soda syphon but it is now empty. He cannot see another one on the table, but remembers where they are kept. He puts down his glass and goes to the cupboard behind the armchair. He moves the chair out of the way, opens the door and the limp body of a man falls out into his astonished arms

Andrew, Jane and Sarah enter in the garden talking happily, oblivious of Geoff's predicament

Geoff staggers a little under the weight of his burden, wondering what the hell to do

Andrew Your glass looks very empty, Sarah.

Sarah (*feigning surprise*) Oh—yes, Andrew, I believe it is.

Andrew Time for one more before dinner, I think.
Sarah What a good idea!

Andrew goes towards the house. Geoff is still undecided what to do with his unwelcome load. Andrew pauses on the way

Andrew How about you, Jane?
Jane Not for me, thank you, darling.
Andrew Right.

Geoff pushes the body back into the cupboard, closes the door hurriedly and is leaning against it, breathless and shaken, as Andrew comes in from the garden. He picks up the bottle of gin and a tonic and then sees Geoff

You'd better have another drink, Geoff. You look as if you've seen a ghost.

Andrew starts to go back into the garden, leaving Geoff stunned
Black-out

the CURTAIN *falls*

SCENE 2

The same. The following morning

It is a lovely day. The sun shining and the birds singing serenely. A peaceful English scene. The ladder has now been removed

Geoff comes in from the hall. He is carrying his week-end grip and is making furtively for the garden. He goes outside and is about to make his escape when Sally rounds the corner of the house and sees him

Sally Geoff!

Geoff jumps a mile

Geoff Aaah! (*He turns nervously to look at her*)
Sally Where are you going?
Geoff (*stammering*) A-a-a-am I going somewhere?
Sally Well, you've got your bag with you.

He looks at his bag in some surprise

Geoff Oh—*this*? Yes. Yes, I packed it. Last night. After dinner.
Sally (*disappointedly*) So you're going?
Geoff Yes.
Sally What!

He puts his bag down and moves closer to her

Geoff (*miserably*) Look—I've been awake all night. Couldn't sleep a wink. Just kept thinking. And now I've made up my mind and I'm leaving.
Sally Why?
Geoff Because you said the window-cleaner was the last. And he wasn't.
Sally Well, there hasn't been one since.

Geoff paces away distractedly to below the garden seat

Geoff Oh, yes, there has. I *saw* him!
Sally Saw who?

He turns

Geoff One of *them*!

Sally goes to him, trying hard not to laugh

Sally (*in mock horror*) Not a . . .?
Geoff Yes.
Sally Dead?
Geoff Well, he didn't have much to say for himself!
Sally Where?
Geoff In there! In the cupboard. I went to get some soda and there he was.
Sally Why?
Geoff What?
Sally Why did you want some soda?
Geoff Because I felt like another whisky, so I poured myself one and there wasn't any soda and I do need soda with whisky and . . . (*He breaks off*) Sally, the soda isn't important. I never found the soda, anyway . . .
Sally So you had your whisky neat?
Geoff Yes.
Sally (*looking towards the house*) I'm sure there's some in the cupboard. Daddy always—
Geoff Sal—Sal, I'm not concerned about the soda.
Sally Aren't you?
Geoff No. No—I stopped looking for the soda because I found . . . something else.
Sally Oh, don't be so silly. You must have imagined it.

He goes to her urgently

Geoff He fell out of the cupboard right into my arms!
Sally So what did you do with him?
Geoff (*angrily*) What do you think I did with him? The tango?
Sally There's no need to get cross.
Geoff (*quieter*) I just—put him back in the cupboard.

Sally reacts in mock alarm, sending him up

Sally You mean—he's still *in* there?
Geoff Well, of course he's still in there! You don't expect him to get up and walk away, do you?

She smiles, amused by his wild imaginings

Sally (*casually*) Let's go and have a look at him, then.
Geoff (*surprised*) Don't you *mind*?
Sally Well, we'll have to find out who he is, won't we?
Geoff (*wildly*) Ask your parents! I'm sure *they* know all about it!
Sally (*sweetly*) Now you're just being silly. (*As to a child*) Come along, darling.

She takes him by the hand and leads him into the house and across to the cupboard. He hesitates

Geoff Sal—are you sure you *want* to look at him? A dead body's not a very nice sight, you know.
Sally (*blasé*) We *have* had them before.

With a tolerant smile, Sally opens the cupboard door. No sign of a body. She takes a soda syphon out of the cupboard and gives him a patient smile

Dead body? Looks more like a soda syphon to me. (*She hands the syphon to him abruptly*) There you are!

Geoff goes and peers into the cupboard anxiously. He turns back to Sally, puzzled

Geoff He was there last night . . .
Sally Well, if he was there last night where is he now?
Geoff *I* don't know! But he was there all right. I'll find him! And then you'll *have* to believe me!
Sally (*trying hard to be patient*) And where do you think you're going to find him?
Geoff I dunno, but he can't have gone far! (*He goes quickly towards the hall*)

Andrew comes in from the hall, dressed for gardening with wellington boots on. He is carrying the morning paper. He sees the soda syphon that Geoff is still carrying

Andrew Good lord! Are you drinking already?

Geoff realizes he still has the soda syphon, hands it quickly to Andrew and rushes out into the hall

What's the matter with him?
Sally He didn't sleep very well.
Andrew Oh. Poor chap. (*He puts down the soda syphon and wanders towards the window seat*) Something on his mind?

Sally gives him an old-fashioned look

Sally Yes, Daddy.
Andrew Oh—yes. Yes, of course.

They chuckle together

Pity he had to find out. I must say, though, I think he's being awfully
selfish about it. A bit of sympathy wouldn't come amiss. (*Looking out of
the window*) Have we got a visitor?
Sally No. Why?
Andrew There's a bag in the garden.
Sally It's Geoff's.
Andrew (*brightening visibly*) Oh, is he leaving?
Sally I think so.
Andrew Going to West Hartlepool?
Sally No, Daddy!
Andrew Oh. Well, I suppose he wants to make a start on those walls of
his. (*He sits on the sofa*)

Pause. Andrew looks at the newspaper

Sally Daddy . . . there hasn't been *another* accident, has there? *Since* the
window-cleaner.
Andrew No, of course not.
Sally I knew it must be his imagination.
Andrew H'm?
Sally He said he found something in that cupboard last night.
Andrew (*engrossed in his newspaper*) Oh, yes . . .?
Sally He wanted some soda to have with his whisky but he couldn't find
any.
Andrew Found the whisky all right, though.
Sally Yes, he did.
Andrew Yes, he would.
Sally But the soda was finished.
Andrew So he had to have it neat? Well, I expect that's what did it. I
mean, if you're only used to drinking that apple stuff neat whisky's
bound to be a bit of a shock to the system.

Sally sits beside him

Sally Daddy—he said there was something *in* the cupboard.
Andrew Yes. There is. Tonic water and bitter lemon. He should have had
some of that.
Sally A man.

Andrew looks up from his newspaper

Andrew A man in the cupboard?
Sally That's what he says.

Andrew chuckles at the absurdity of it

Andrew What was he doing in there?
Sally Not a lot. He was dead.
Andrew Don't be silly, darling.
Sally Geoff says that when he opened the door a body fell out.

Andrew glances apprehensively towards the whisky

Andrew How much of my whisky did he have last night?

They both laugh

Geoff comes in from the hall, heading for the garden

Geoff I'm going to look in the garden.
Andrew You won't find him out there, either!

Andrew and Sally laugh. Geoff goes urgently to Andrew

Geoff Where have you hidden him?

This only makes Andrew and Sally laugh even more

Andrew I should stick to apple juice in future.

Geoff goes to the cupboard in great agitation

Geoff I opened that door and there he was! I was looking for a soda syphon.

Jane appears in the garden, returning from the shops. She sees Geoff's bag

I don't know how you can take it so calmly.
Andrew Well, I'm sorry, but I never could get awfully worked up over soda water. I'm a Malvern man myself.

Jane comes in from the garden with her shopping

Jane I say, did you know that there's a bag out there in the garden?
Andrew }(*together*) It's *his*!
Sally
Jane It'll get awfully wet if it rains. (*She puts her shopping down*)
Sally He's not leaving it there, Mummy.
Jane Oh, good. I wouldn't like anyone to trip over it. Andrew, I've been awfully extravagant. I bought some fresh salmon for dinner tonight.
Andrew Well, don't let *him* know or he'll change his mind about leaving.
Sally Daddy . . .!

Jane looks across at Geoff

Jane Oh? Aren't you staying for the week-end, then, Geoff?
Geoff I'm afraid not. (*Heavily*) I may have to tell the police . . .
Jane (*puzzled*) Would they be interested?
Geoff Tell them what I found in the cupboard!

Jane looks inquiringly at Andrew

Andrew He seems to think it's a criminal offence to store tonic water and bitter lemon.
Geoff You know very well what I'm talking about! (*He turns to Jane*) Last night there was a dead man in that cupboard.
Jane Really? Good heavens! I *am* surprised. (*She goes thoughtfully to the cupboard*) But if he was dead how did he get *into* the cupboard? (*To Sally*) What's he talking about?

Sally After hearing about Mr Merry his imagination's running riot.

Geoff goes urgently to Andrew

Geoff What are we going to do?

Andrew rises

Andrew Well, *I'm* going to do a little digging.

Geoff reacts and looks at him in horror

Geoff Getting ready for the Vicar?

They all look at him, more than a little surprised at this outburst

Sally (*wearily*) Geoff, will you stop going on about the clergy?
Geoff (*desperately*) But something's got to be done!
Andrew You've already done all there is to be done. (*He advances on Geoff, occasionally striking him on the chest with his newspaper and forcing him to back away to the armchair*) You haven't shown us the slightest sympathy in spite of our sharing our secrets with you. You've gone prying into my private cupboard, drunk more than your share of my whisky, and now you've packed your toothbrush and you're off to live in a collapsing house with no water. (*He gives Geoff a push, causing him to sit on the chair*) Well, I'm going into the garden. (*He makes for the garden*)
Geoff (*loudly*) I'm *going* to tell them! I've *got* to tell them!

Andrew stops and turns

Andrew Who?
Geoff The police, of course!
Andrew (*calmly*) Well, go ahead. Tell them. Nobody's stopping you.

Geoff rises in surprise

Geoff Aren't they?
Andrew Of course not. If it'll make you any happier, you go and tell the police. Constable Burgoyne—he's the chap you want. He's been here before. But he will want to see the body, you know. He won't just take your word for it.
Geoff All right. I'll find it! It was here, so I'll find it! Just a matter of time. You wait and see!

Geoff rushes out into the garden, trips over his bag, swears, collects himself and disappears down the garden

Andrew I don't think planting cabbages is doing Geoff any good. (*He looks out of the window*)
Jane I don't think you can blame him, Andrew. After all, it must have been a bit of a shock to find out about the accident rate in this house.
Andrew That's no reason for him to start imagining there are bodies lying about in cupboards. If anyone else *had* had an accident and dropped dead, I'd simply have dialled nine-nine-nine in the usual way and they'd

have sent an ambulance to collect him. He's simply over-reacting to the whole thing.

Jane (*thoughtfully*) You don't think we ought to put up a few notices?

Andrew What sort of notices?

Jane Well—to warn people about the hazards.

Andrew Like a sign at the top of the stairs saying "Danger—Steep Hill"? (*He chuckles*)

Geoff is heard calling excitedly from down the garden

Geoff (*off*) Quick! Quick! Come here—all of you!

Geoff comes running in from the garden and races into the sitting-room

Andrew *Now* what's he found?

Geoff Come on! All of you! Hurry up! Outside! Quick!

Andrew Is the house on fire?

Geoff I did it! I did it!

Jane What?

Geoff I knew I would!

Andrew Pull yourself together, man! (*He strikes Geoff on the chest with his newspaper*)

Geoff I found him!

Jane Who?

Geoff The one in there!

Sally But there isn't anyone in there!

Geoff No. Not any more. Because he's out there!

Sally What?

Andrew Don't be ridiculous.

Geoff He's outside! I knew he would be!

Jane Geoff dear, do try to calm down . . .

Geoff I told you I'd find him and I did! He's out there now! Floating in the lily pond! Come and look!

Geoff grabs the astonished Sally and drags her off into the garden. They stumble over the bag, collect themselves and run off down the garden

Andrew I do wish he'd move that damn bag. Somebody'll break their neck on it soon. (*He sits on the sofa*)

Jane (*on her way*) Aren't you coming?

Andrew Whatever for? You don't really believe him, do you? He's imagining things.

Jane All the same, I think we ought to go and see, Andrew.

Andrew Now don't *you* start! Dead bodies don't get into lily ponds without any help, you know.

Jane But he might have fallen in. And if someone *is* in there we'll have to get him out. He'll poison the fish.

Jane goes out into the garden, avoids the bag at the last minute and disappears down the garden

Andrew starts to read the morning paper

Sarah comes in from the hall

Sarah I've been very spoilt. Had my breakfast in bed. Two boiled eggs and orange juice. Delicious. Why have you got your boots on?
Andrew (*engrossed in his newspaper*) I'm gardening.
Sarah Sorry?
Andrew Thought I'd do a bit of digging. Such a lovely morning.
Sarah All the same, you shouldn't wear your boots in the house. You'll get mud all over the carpet. (*She goes to look out of the window*)
Andrew I'm going out, not coming in.
Sarah (*looking into the garden*) What are they doing out there?
Andrew (*casually*) Geoff seems to think he's found a body floating in the lily pond.

Sarah remembers something

Sarah Good heavens! I'd forgotten all about him . . .!
Andrew (*reading*) H'm?
Sarah It completely slipped my memory.
Andrew What did?
Sarah The one out there in the pond.

Andrew looks up

Andrew What are you talking about?
Sarah The man in the lily pond.
Andrew You mean to say there really *is* someone out there?
Sarah Oh, yes. Well, he was there last night.

Andrew considers this for a moment

Andrew How do *you* know?
Sarah Because I put him there.

A pause. He just looks at her

Andrew In the lily pond?
Sarah Yes.
Andrew You put him there?
Sarah Last night. After dinner.
Andrew Don't be silly. You couldn't have done that.
Sarah Why not? He was only small. (*Reasonably*) Well, *you* were all washing up. So I put him in the wheelbarrow, took him out and tipped him in.
Andrew Took him out and tipped him in?
Sarah Yes.
Andrew Why?
Sarah Well, I couldn't very well leave him in here, could I? Do be sensible. (*She goes out into the garden*)

Andrew thinks for a moment, then gets up and goes outside

Andrew (*baffled*) Sarah—I wish I could understand what you're talking about. You mean there really *is* a dead man in our lily pond?

Sarah Yes.

Andrew And where was he before that?

Sarah Before the lily pond?

Andrew Yes.

Sarah In the wheelbarrow.

Andrew (*patiently*) No, no, Sarah. No. Before the wheelbarrow. I mean—where did you *get* him from?

Sarah Oh! From in there. From in the cupboard.

Andrew So Geoff was right? It wasn't just tonic water and bitter lemon?

Sarah You mean Geoff had already *seen* him in the cupboard?

Andrew Apparently. Before dinner.

Sarah (*a bit put out*) Oh, dear. I could have left him where he was then.

A pause. Andrew thinks for a moment

Andrew Sarah, I keep getting confused . . .

Sarah Well, I didn't want to leave him in that cupboard in case you went to get something out of it and Geoff saw him.

Andrew What if he did? What difference would it make?

Sarah Well, he was so upset when he heard about all the others, I didn't want to make him any *more* agitated. I know *you* don't like him, but we do—and the poor boy was in such a state about Mr Merry and the others—well, I thought one more would be enough to send him rushing off to West Hartlepool or somewhere.

Andrew Very good thing, too!

Sarah Andrew, that's very naughty. Sometimes you seem to forget that Sally loves him. Anyway, I thought he'd be less conspicuous in the pond.

Andrew It's only eighteen inches deep.

Sarah (*a little cross*) Well, I'd forgotten! (*She sits on the garden seat*) Anyway, that's where I put him.

Andrew Good lord. You poor darling. (*He sits beside her*) Why on earth didn't you call me? I'd have given you a hand.

Sarah But you were helping with the washing-up.

Andrew Let's get out priorities right, shall we, Sarah? The washing-up could have waited.

Sarah Oh, no. Jane always likes to get it out of the way before we have coffee.

Andrew There were plenty of people to do the washing-up. You should have called me. (*Pause*) What were you after in there, anyway? Tonic water or bitter lemon?

Sarah What do you mean?

Andrew When you opened the cupboard door and found him.

Sarah Oh, I *knew* he was in the cupboard all the time.

Andrew looks at her blankly for a moment

Andrew You knew he was in the cupboard all the time.

Sarah Well, of course! I *put* him there.

Andrew You put him there?

Sarah Yesterday afternoon.

Andrew Yesterday afternoon! Why?

Sarah just looks at him blankly, so he persists

Why did you put him in the cupboard?

Sarah (*logically*) Well, I didn't want to leave him lying about the place in case somebody called. So I popped him in the cupboard for the time being. (*Quite annoyed*) I did *try* to tell you before dinner, but you were all talking and then I forgot. You know what my memory's like, Andrew.

Andrew considers for a moment

Andrew Look, when you . . . popped him in the cupboard—was he already dead?

Sarah (*with a laugh*) I'd have had a bit of a struggle if he'd been alive!

Andrew gets up in confusion and moves away

Andrew Sarah . . . Sarah, I'm still a little confused. Why didn't you simply telephone the police? They'd have sent an ambulance to collect him.

Sarah Oh, I did. I asked for Constable Burgoyne just as we always do. But he wasn't there.

Andrew Presumably the police station had not been left unmanned?

Sarah No, of course not. But those other officers are such dreadful gossips, Andrew. Tell *them* and it'll be around the village in no time. I thought I'd wait until Mr Burgoyne was back. He's so much more sympathetic.

Andrew (*resignedly*) I see . . . Who *was* he, anyway?

Sarah Who?

Andrew (*patiently*) The one you took out and tipped in.

Sarah Oh. Television repair man.

Andrew (*his hackles rising*) The T.V. repair man? You mean to say he was here yesterday afternoon?

Sarah Yes.

Andrew I distinctly told them—mornings only! Now we'll miss all the highlights of the cricket. (*He goes into the house grumpily*) Well, all I can say is, they'd jolly well better come again on Monday or they can have the wretched set back again!

Sarah follows him indoors

Sarah Andrew . . .

Andrew What?

Sarah (*pointedly*) I'm not sure that they'll be too keen to call again.

Andrew What? (*He realizes*) Oh. Yes. Yes, I see what you mean. Well, go on, then. What happened?

Sarah Well, I let him in, showed him in here and left him to get on with it. (*Thoughtfully, moving to the window seat*) I suppose there must have been a slow circuit or something.

Andrew Short.

Sarah What?

Andrew Short circuit.

Sarah Oh, really? Anyhow, when I came back in here to see how he was getting on he was lying down over there.

Andrew Dead?

Sarah Oh, yes. (*Thoughtfully*) You know, Andrew—perhaps you should have put a notice on the television set saying "Danger--Electricity".

Andrew (*patiently*) Sarah . . . he was a television repair man. They're supposed to know all about electricity. You poor darling. Must have given you a terrible shock.

Sarah Not as much as it gave him!

Andrew And that was when you put him in the cupboard?

Sarah Yes.

Andrew (*wearily*) Oh, well, I'd better give the police another ring. See if Constable Burgoyne's back yet. (*He starts for the telephone*)

Before he can do so, Jane comes quickly in from the garden

Jane Andrew! Andrew, you'll have to do something! (*She goes to the hall and gets her Wellington boots*)

Andrew Will I?

Jane (*returning*) Geoff was quite right. There *is* someone in the lily pond. You can see him quite clearly. Slightly submerged under the pond weed. (*She goes out into the garden, sits on the garden chair and starts to put her boots on*)

Andrew (*to Sarah*) He must be very thin. It's only eighteen inches deep.

They go out into the garden to join Jane

Andrew What am *I* supposed to do about it?

Jane You'll have to get him out.

Andrew Start wading about in the middle of the pond?

Jane You've got your boots on.

Andrew They're for gardening.

Jane Darling, we can't leave him out there.

Andrew Why not? The police can drag him out when they get here. That's what they're paid for! (*He sits on the garden seat*)

Jane Darling, you know what the police are like in this village. Half the time they're half asleep.

Sarah And the rest of the time they're *fast* asleep.

Jane By the time they get here it'll be tea-time.

Andrew What's that got to do with it?

Jane Somebody might call in for tea.

Sarah Yes, Andrew, they often do on a Saturday.

Jane And they're bound to want to look at the goldfish. They'd think it a bit odd if they looked down into the water and saw someone looking back up at them.

Andrew has an idea

Andrew We could say it was your cousin from Alfriston. He's very fond of underwater swimming. (*He mimes the breast stroke*)

Jane Don't be so silly, Andrew. We'll have to get him out.

Andrew Well, let Geoff get him out. He's a lot stronger than I am.

Jane Well, Geoff's in a bit of a state at the moment. He really does over-react so dreadfully, doesn't he? Sally's gone chasing after him round the garden trying to calm him down. (*She rises decisively*) So you see, Andrew, there's no choice. You'll have to help. (*Thoughtfully*) I wonder who the poor man was. Fancy falling in the pond and drowning like that.

Andrew He didn't drown.

Jane Well, if he didn't he's holding his breath for a very long time. (*She starts to go*)

Sarah (*suddenly*) Good heavens! I'd almost forgotten.

Jane stops

Andrew Sarah, I wish you'd stop forgetting things. What is it now?

Sarah The Vicar. He telephoned just after breakfast. You were both in the garden so I answered it upstairs. (*Delightedly*) He's coming to see you.

Andrew Oh, God!

Sarah No. Just the Vicar.

Jane When is he coming?

Sarah This morning.

Jane (*horrified*) This morning?!

Sarah (*innocently*) Isn't it convenient?

Jane returns to Sarah

Jane Not really. We've got a dead body floating in the lily pond. Whatever will he think of us?

Andrew What does it matter what he thinks of us? The Vicar must have seen a dead body before now. Ashes to ashes. All that sort of thing.

Jane I know, darling, but I do want to get off on the right foot with the new Vicar. First impressions are very important. After all, we shall want him to marry Sally.

Andrew Why the hell should he want to marry Sally?

Jane Sally and Geoff!

Andrew Oh, I see. (*He reacts*) Over my dead body!

Sarah Andrew, please don't say things like that. (*She sits on the garden chair*)

Jane And if he gets to know that we're accident prone he may not perform the ceremony.

Andrew Why not?

Jane (*as if to a child*) In case he trips over her train and breaks his neck. You know how impressionable people are. So come along, Andrew— we'll have to get him out. (*She pulls him to his feet*)

Andrew (*reluctantly*) I was just going to see to the garden. Do a bit of digging.

Jane You can do that later. Oh, come *on*, Andrew! (*She urges him on*)

Andrew (*grumbling*) Well, where are we going to put him? Back in the cupboard again?

Jane What cupboard?

Andrew (*after a glance at Sarah*) Never mind. It's a long story.

Jane Put him in the summer house. And lock the door!
Andrew There's no need for that. He won't be trying to get out.

Andrew goes off down the garden

Jane You know, sometimes I think Andrew has got no sense of occasion.
Sarah Well, men don't seem to care about keeping up appearances like we do. Mind you, it is a shame about the cricket.
Jane (*puzzled*) Cricket?
Sarah Still, I suppose he could go and see it next door . . .

The front door bell rings. Sarah rises quickly

Jane Good heavens! He can't be here already, can he?
Sarah He said just before lunch.
Jane Well, we aren't expecting anyone else.
Sarah Probably the milkman wanting his money.
Jane Yes, of course!
Sarah I'll go.

Sarah goes out into the hall

Jane starts to go into the garden with her boots on

Andrew (*off*) Come on!
Jane (*going*) All right, Andrew. There's no need to shout.

Jane goes off down the garden. Geoff and Sally appear from up the garden. She is now wearing yellow wellingtons

Sally All right, Geoff. There's no need to shout.
Geoff I wasn't shouting! I just want to know how he *got* into the lily pond. Is that so unreasonable?
Sally Well, he must have fallen in, mustn't he? And just when I thought our luck was changing!
Geoff (*tense*) Sal—he was in there. In the cupboard. So somebody must have moved him!
Sally Don't be so silly. Why should anyone want to go trundling a dead body in and out? Honestly, I don't know what's come over you. I knew you shouldn't have started drinking whisky. (*She starts to go*)
Geoff Where are you going?
Sally Where do you think? To help my father move the body!

Sally sails off down the garden

Geoff watches her go, dazed and dumbfounded. He sinks on to the garden seat, a broken man

Inside the house, a slightly apprehensive Sarah comes in from the hall

Sarah Perhaps you'd like to wait in here?

The Vicar comes in from the hall wearing a nondescript suit, a clerical collar and bicycle clips. He carries his hat

Vicar I hope I haven't called at a bad moment.

Sarah Well, they are rather busy. Seeing to something in the garden.

Vicar (*smiling*) Ah! Flora?

Sarah No. Fauna. So if you prefer to come back another time . . .

Vicar Well, I would sooner wait if it's all the same to you. I'll just sit here until they've finished whatever it is they're doing. (*He sits down*) It'll give me time to catch my breath. It's quite a long way to pedal up here, you know.

Sarah Oh. Well, in that case, perhaps you'd like a cup of coffee?

Vicar That would be very nice. Thank you.

Sarah Sugar?

Vicar Three, please. I have a very sweet tooth.

Sarah Three. Right. I shan't be a moment.

Sarah smiles and goes out into the hall

The Vicar settles down to wait

In the garden, Geoff glances briefly towards the house and back again. A pause, then he reacts to what he has seen. An unsuspecting vicar on a sofa! He looks again to make sure that his eyes have not deceived him and reacts with fearful apprehension. He gets up quickly and rushes into the house, tripping over his bag as he does so. The Vicar looks up in surprise as a distraught young man comes in from the garden and gazes at him in horror

Geoff What the hell are *you* doing here?

Black-out

the CURTAIN *falls*

ACT II

SCENE 1

The same. The action is continuous

The Vicar is looking rather surprised. Geoff is gazing at him in horrified apprehension

Geoff What the hell are *you* doing here?
Vicar I was told to wait.
Geoff What for?
Vicar Er—coffee.
Geoff Coffee?!
Vicar Is anything wrong?
Geoff (*crossing below the Vicar*) I wouldn't drink the coffee if I were you. Not in *this* house.
Vicar Instant?
Geoff More than likely!
Vicar That's all right. I don't mind. I always use it myself. Never bother with the beans.
Geoff You're new here, aren't you?
Vicar Yes. I've never been before. It's a very nice house, isn't it?
Geoff I mean new to the village.
Vicar Oh. Yes.
Geoff That's what I heard. (*He paces grimly below the Vicar again*)
Vicar Oh—you've heard about me?
Geoff Yes. They were talking about you.
Vicar (*pleased*) Really?

Geoff sits beside the Vicar and speaks confidentially

Geoff You've—you've heard about the window-cleaner?
Vicar Oh, yes. (*Pause*) But I'm sure it's all lies.

Geoff looks puzzled

Geoff What did you hear about him?
Vicar Well, one or two people thought he was spending too much time at Mrs Glasspool's. More time than her windows warranted. You know what I mean?
Geoff (*blankly*) No.
Vicar Well—her husband is away. In Africa.
Geoff But he's dead!
Vicar Mr Glasspool?
Geoff No, no. The window-cleaner.

Vicar Really? I never knew that. I don't recall the ceremony. Oh, dear.
Don't tell me that Mr Glasspool returned unexpectedly?

Geoff (*bewildered*) He fell off his ladder and broke his neck!

Vicar Mr Glasspool?

Geoff The window-cleaner!

Vicar (*puzzled*) But I saw him yesterday. Hardly seemed the worse for wear.

Geoff Oh, you must be talking about the *new* window-cleaner. I think I meant the *old* one.

Vicar Oh. I see . . . (*But he looks puzzled*)

Sarah comes round the corner of the house to attract the attention of Andrew and Jane, but being a bit vague about the geography of the house is unaware that the Vicar can now see her. She calls down the garden in an elaborate whisper

Sarah Andrew . . .! Jane . . .!

The Vicar and Geoff turn and see her. The Vicar is rather surprised to see her there

Vicar That's the lady who let me in. She *said* she was getting me coffee.

Sarah He's here!

A muffled reply from down the garden

The Vicar! He's here!

Sarah turns and sees the Vicar and Geoff. She smiles, feeling awkward

The coffee won't be long.

Sarah disappears round to the front of the house again

The Vicar smiles nervously, somewhat surprised by the behaviour pattern of the residents

Geoff Why did you come here?

Vicar Well, I like to meet all my new parishioners. You never know. They may be in need of help.

Geoff I doubt it! They seem to be managing all right. Are they expecting you?

Vicar Oh, yes. I telephoned and said I'd be popping along.

Geoff (*alarmed*) You haven't come to tea, have you?

Vicar I'd be a little early for that, wouldn't I? Perhaps another time.

Geoff I wouldn't come to tea if I were you!

Vicar (*with a smile*) Well, I wasn't banking on it.

Geoff No, but *they* were!

Vicar Sorry? I don't understand . . .

Geoff (*rising*) I wouldn't stay if I were you. I'll tell them you called. (*He tries to pull the astonished Vicar to his feet*)

Vicar What on earth . . .?

Geoff Get out of here while you've still got the chance!

Vicar But I've only just arrived.

Andrew, Jane and Sally appear in the garden. He is pushing a wheelbarrow in which is the limp body of the television repair man. They are talking to each other and do not see who is indoors

Jane Are you sure you can manage, darling?
Andrew Of course I can manage. Do stop fussing.

Andrew puts the wheelbarrow down to take a breather. Geoff sees them, reacts with alarm, turns to the Vicar and stands directly in front of him, his arms up in the air to prevent him seeing out into the garden. The Vicar, naturally, cannot understand what the hell is going on. He looks for a while at Geoff, increasingly puzzled. Geoff smiles back, nervously

Vicar (*eventually*) What are you doing?

Geoff cannot think what he is doing

Geoff I'm—I'm reaching!
Vicar Reaching?
Geoff Yes. Reaching up to heaven!

The Vicar smiles, deeply impressed

Vicar How very nice.

In the garden, Andrew, Jane and Sally continue on their way, bearing the burden in the barrow and talking as they go. They disappear up the garden

Geoff glances over his shoulder to try to see if they have gone. He wants to make sure so he starts to back slowly towards the window, his arms still aloft. The Vicar watches, intrigued

Vicar What are you doing now?
Geoff What?
Vicar You're walking backwards.
Geoff Yes. Yes, I'm reaching up to heaven and walking backwards. Both at the same time.
Vicar I've never seen *that* done before.

Geoff makes sure all is clear and then lowers his arms

Geoff (*with a nervous laugh*) That's all right. All over. (*He returns to the Vicar*) Does anyone know you're here?
Vicar Er—I don't think so. Why?
Geoff You didn't leave word with the Curate?
Vicar No.
Geoff Worse than I thought!
Vicar What *are* you talking about?
Geoff I'll have to get you out of here somehow.
Vicar It's quite all right. I've got my bicycle outside.
Geoff They might see you.

Vicar (*modestly*) That doesn't matter. I ride tolerably well.

Geoff You don't think they'd let you go? Not now you're here.

Vicar Well, I'm sure they're very hospitable, but I do have other parishioners.

Geoff They won't let *you* get away!

Vicar What?

Geoff I overheard them talking. They think you know about the window-cleaner.

Vicar Oh, I see. And they're friends of Mr Glasspool?

Geoff What? Look, there's no time to explain! Do as I say and you'll be quite all right. Come on—over here!

Geoff pulls the astonished Vicar to his feet and leads him by the hand to the cupboard

Vicar Where are we going?

Geoff You'll soon see.

Geoff moves the chair out of the way and opens the cupboard

You wait in there.

Vicar What?

Geoff Do as I say! I'll tell you when it's all clear to come out.

Vicar Look, I don't understand. When a vicar comes to call . . . (*He mumbles despondently*)

Geoff There's no time to argue! In you go.

Geoff pushes the Vicar into the cupboard and closes the door. From within we hear the sound of ecclesiastical outrage. Geoff opens the door again and the Vicar emerges, still talking

Vicar It's really very unusual to treat a member of the. . . .

Geoff (*rather cross*) This door isn't soundproof, you know. Keep the noise down.

Vicar But it's dark in there!

Geoff You're not going to be reading. Concentrate on next Sunday's sermon.

Geoff pushes the Vicar back in and closes the door again. He replaces the chair and sits on it

Sarah comes in from the hall with a cup of coffee. She arrives at the sofa before realizing that the Vicar is no longer where he was. She peers uncomprehendingly at the empty place on the sofa

Sarah Oh, dear . . . You—you haven't seen a vicar, have you?

Geoff I saw one in church once. Easter Sunday it was. A lot of flowers.

Sarah No. I meant—in here.

Geoff Oh. No.

Puzzled, Sarah looks towards the window. The Vicar pushes the cupboard door open on to the back of the chair. Geoff hastily closes it before Sarah turns back to him again

Sarah (*totally bemused*) I'm sure there was one here a moment ago . . .
Geoff A vicar?
Sarah Yes. I went to get him some coffee. He was sitting just there.
Geoff On the sofa?
Sarah Yes.
Geoff *I* didn't see him.

Sarah drifts in puzzlement towards the window. The Vicar pushes the door open again. Geoff hastily shuts it. Sarah turns to Geoff again

Sarah Wait a minute, though. When I was out there I saw him in here with you.
Geoff Oh? Was that a *vicar*?
Sarah Well, you must have noticed his collar.

The Vicar peers out of the cupboard: an event which Sarah does not appear to think in any way unusual. She smiles delightedly. The Vicar waves self-consciously

Ah, there you are! (*To Geoff*) You see? I knew I wasn't mistaken.
Geoff Oh—*this* vicar? I didn't know you meant *this* one.

Geoff allows the Vicar into the room

Sarah (*to the Vicar, suddenly realizing*) What were you doing in the cupboard?
Vicar Waiting for coffee.
Sarah You didn't have to wait in a cupboard. I left you sitting on the sofa.
Vicar Yes, I know, but you see . . .
Geoff He's very interested in cupboards. Aren't you, Vicar? He wants to build one like it at home.

Sarah gives him a doubtful look and then turns again to the Vicar

Sarah Now then, you come back and sit down here . . .
Vicar Thank you so much. (*He sits on the sofa and accepts the cup of coffee from Sarah*) Oh. That looks nice and strong.
Sarah Yes. I made it specially. And three spoonfuls of sugar just as you said.
Vicar How very kind of you.

Sarah moves away to the window seat. Geoff watches as the Vicar stirs his coffee and then lifts the cup to his lips

Geoff (*alarmed*) No!

The Vicar stops, the coffee poised

Vicar What?
Geoff Do you think you should have coffee? It'll keep you awake.
Vicar As it's only the middle of the morning I don't imagine I shall find that too distressing. (*He tries again to start his coffee*)
Geoff Wouldn't you like to go for a walk?

Vicar Well—I *was* just going to have my coffee. Later perhaps?
Geoff It might be *too* late, then!

Again the Vicar attempts his coffee

  Just a minute! May I?

*The astonished Vicar cannot understand why a strange young man is now
taking his coffee away from him*

Vicar What *are* you doing?
Geoff Might not be sweet enough for you.

*Geoff goes round above the sofa, with the coffee going cold and the Vicar
getting hot*

Vicar (*following Geoff*) Will you please give me back my coffee?

Geoff arrives in front of Sarah and offers her the cup of coffee

Geoff *You* try it!
Vicar I may only be a clergyman but I'm perfectly capable of trying my
  own coffee!
Geoff No. She made it, so she can try it.
Sarah (*patiently*) Well, of course, Geoff. If it'll make you any happier.
  But I wish I knew what this is all about. (*She takes a sip of the coffee*)
  H'm. Far too sweet for me, of course. (*She gives it back to Geoff*)
Geoff (*surprised*) You tried it!
Sarah Well, you asked me to. (*She sits on the window seat*)
Geoff Yes, but I didn't think you would. (*To the Vicar*) I didn't think
  she would and she did . . .

*Geoff unconsciously goes to drink the coffee, realizes his mistake, hands the
cup back to the Vicar and drifts away in a daze. The Vicar is beginning to
wish he was at a christening*

Vicar Thank you.

*The Vicar sits down and at long last is allowed to make a start on his cup
of coffee*

  *At this moment Jane, Andrew and Sally come in from the garden, chatter-
  ing. They stop when they see the Vicar sitting on the sofa*

Andrew Good lord! We're not ready for *you* yet!
Sarah Andrew—the Vicar's arrived.
Andrew So he has.
Sarah He's come for coffee.
Andrew Well, he's got some, hasn't he, so that's all right.
Vicar (*smiling*) It was a little too early for tea.
Andrew What a pity. (*To Sally*) What's he talking about?
Sally I don't know.

Jane goes to the Vicar and sits beside him, all gracious and charming

Jane Vicar—what a *lovely* surprise!

Andrew and Sally look at each other and giggle

Vicar (*to Jane*) I beg your pardon?
Jane You being here like this. An unexpected pleasure.
Vicar Well, I did telephone.
Jane Oh, yes. I didn't mean we didn't *know*. I meant we didn't know *when*.
Sarah But I called out to you in the garden.
Andrew Oh, is that what you were saying, Sarah? We couldn't understand.
Vicar What were you doing in the garden?
Andrew Getting rid of the rubbish.

Geoff looks alarmed and goes abruptly to the Vicar, leaning across Jane to speak to him

Geoff How about that walk now?
Vicar What?
Andrew Why should he want to go for a walk? (*To the Vicar*) You're not overweight, are you?
Vicar Ten stone six.
Andrew Just as I thought. A modest weight.
Vicar I keep fit on my bicycle.
Andrew Is that how you came here? On a bicycle?
Vicar Yes.
Andrew (*to Sally*) He came on a bicycle. I wish I'd seen that. How splendid.

Sally giggles and sits on the window seat next to Sarah

Geoff Three spoonfuls of sugar!
Andrew What?
Geoff That's what he had.
Andrew On his bicycle?
Geoff In his coffee.
Andrew Three spoonfuls?
Vicar My only vice.
Andrew I should hope so.
Geoff So after three spoonfuls of sugar I'm sure you need a walk. A bit of exercise.
Vicar Well, I . . .
Geoff You like gardens, don't you?
Vicar Certainly.
Geoff Then you'll want to see the phlox and the hollyhocks—(*pointedly*) on your way out.
Vicar But I haven't finished my coffee yet.
Andrew What does he want to go trotting around the garden for as soon as he arrives?
Geoff (*heavily*) Are you frightened of what he might see?
Andrew Certainly not. Nothing wrong with *my* borders.
Geoff What about the pond?

Vicar (*delighted*) Ah! you have a pond?
Andrew Yes. It's outside. In the garden.
Vicar I love ponds.
Andrew I don't think you'd like this one very much. (*He moves to the armchair*)
Vicar Do you keep it well stocked?
Andrew Off and on, yes.

Geoff moves away to the desk in despair

Vicar Goldfish? All that sort of thing.
Andrew Oh, yes. (*He sits in the armchair*)
Vicar I must have a look. (*He puts his coffee down and starts to get up*)

Sarah jumps up in alarm

Sarah No, you can't! (*She pushes the surprised Vicar back on to the sofa*)
Vicar What?
Sarah Not yet! You can't see it yet. (*She moves anxiously to Andrew*) He can't see it yet. Can he, Andrew?
Andrew (*rising, to Sarah, confidentially*) Oh, yes, he can see the *pond* if he wants to. As long as he doesn't go prowling around the *rest* of the garden.
Vicar Oh, dear. I didn't mean to intrude . . .
Jane (*covering quickly*) You couldn't possibly intrude, Vicar. It's just that we'd rather you saw it when it was all tidy. It's a bit messy at the moment. Isn't it, Andrew?
Andrew Oh, yes. Very messy. (*He wanders above the sofa*)
Sarah You managed to clear out the pond, then, Andrew?
Andrew Oh, yes. We put him in the summer-house. I mean we put it in the summer-house. (*To the Vicar*) The wheelbarrow. After we'd finished with it. Leaves. Barrow full of leaves. Dreadful.
Vicar (*puzzled*) Leaves? In the middle of summer?
Andrew Left over from last year. If *you'd* ever had a pond you'd know what it was like.
Vicar But I *have* got a pond.
Andrew Then you'll know what it's like. Gets very cluttered. Leaves. Old boots. Socks. Things like that. So occasionally you have to take the plunge. So we did. That's why we've got our boots on.
Vicar I did wonder.

Sarah sits in the armchair. Jane turns to the Vicar with a bright smile, determined to change the subject and keep up appearances

Jane Well! How nice of you to call!

Andrew and Sally giggle again. The Vicar looks a little surprised at Jane's over-enthusiasm

Vicar Well, being new to the village I felt I ought to get to know my flock.
Andrew (*to Sally, quietly*) Flock?

Sally That's you, Daddy.
Andrew Oh, is it, really? Good heavens.
Jane And we're delighted to see you! Aren't we, Andrew? Absolutely delighted!
Vicar Oh, good. You see, I thought it would be so nice if we met and had a little talk.
Andrew (*guardedly*) What about?
Vicar Well—about this and that.

Andrew and Jane exchange a look

Andrew This and that?
Vicar Well—you know. Things.
Andrew Things, eh? Then you *have* heard about the window-cleaner?
Vicar (*puzzled*) Well—as it happens—I have. But I didn't come here to talk about *him*.
Andrew Well, that's very thoughtful of you, Vicar. But you mustn't be embarrassed. After all, it could happen to anyone. Even to you.
Geoff (*quietly suffering*) Oh, my God . . .! (*He moves away in despair*)
Vicar Well, as regards the window-cleaner my feeling is that what people do in the privacy of their homes is entirely their own affair.
Andrew Is it?
Vicar Yes, indeed. But obviously *you* think differently about it.
Andrew Do we?
Vicar Well—being friends of Mr Glasspool.

Andrew considers this in silence for a moment. He moves thoughtfully to Jane

Andrew (*quietly, to Jane*) Are we friends of Mr Glasspool?
Jane Apparently.

Andrew considers further. He turns to Sarah

Andrew Who's Mr Glasspool?
Sarah I've never heard of him.
Jane (*to the Vicar*) Ah! I expect the *new* one told you?
Vicar New one?
Jane Window-cleaner. I expect he told you what happened to the old one.
Vicar I'm sorry. I'm a little confused.
Sally You're not the only one.
Vicar You see, what *I* heard I heard from the butcher.
Jane The butcher?
Vicar Yes.
Jane I thought he gave me a funny look over the liver last week.
Vicar I beg your pardon?
Jane We can't get one at all now.
Vicar Butcher?
Jane Window-cleaner.
Vicar Why not?

Jane I suppose he doesn't think it's safe to come here. Not after what happened to the last one.
Vicar Oh, I see! (*He laughs*) But I'm sure you're not a bit like Mrs Glasspool.
Jane (*confused*) Oh, thank you. (*Pause*) What was *she* like?
Vicar Well—anything in trousers, apparently.

A pause. They all look puzzled

Sarah Who's Mrs Glasspool?
Andrew Thank you, Sarah. That's just what *I* was thinking!
Vicar Mind you—it is only what I heard from the butcher.
Andrew Yes, it would be . . .

Andrew and Sarah look at each other and shrug

Vicar I do hope it wasn't inconvenient, my popping in this morning.
Jane No, no. Of course not. Was it, Andrew?
Andrew What?
Jane Inconvenient. The Vicar.
Andrew Oh, no. No, not at all. Mind you, I never guessed. Jane said, "Guess who telephoned!" And I didn't. Did I? But, of course, I'm delighted that you did.
Vicar (*puzzled*) Did?
Andrew What?
Vicar Did what?
Andrew What are you talking about?
Vicar What is it that you're delighted that I did?
Andrew (*to Sally, quietly*) What's the matter with him?
Sarah (*to the Vicar*) I think Andrew meant that he was delighted that you did telephone. (*To Andrew*) That *was* what you meant, wasn't it?
Andrew Yes, of course it was. All right now, Vicar? Understand what we're talking about?
Vicar Oh. Yes. Thank you.
Andrew Good. Now, where was I? Ah—yes. "Wonderful!" That's what I said. "Wonderful! We'd better ask him to tea."

Geoff comes down quickly to the Vicar

Geoff There you are! What did I tell you? They want you to come to tea!
Sally Geoff, will you stop getting so excited?
Jane Of course we want you to come to tea.
Vicar Well, thank you very much.
Andrew Tell you what—as you're here—why don't we have tea now?
Sally At half past eleven?
Andrew Ah. No. I suppose not.
Geoff Thank God for that! (*He retreats again*)
Andrew Another time, perhaps.
Vicar Well, I must say—it's very nice to meet you all. I've seen you in church, of course—
Andrew Oh? When was that? Christmas before last?

Jane (*trying to keep up appearances*) Don't be so silly, Andrew. We're always popping in and out.
Andrew Are we?

Sally and Andrew giggle

Jane Of course we are. (*To the Vicar*) He's so forgetful.
Andrew I hadn't noticed you exactly sprinting into Evensong.
Jane Andrew! (*She gives him a hard look*)
Sarah *This* Vicar wasn't here the Christmas before last.
Andrew That's right.

Geoff makes another desperate attempt to get the Vicar to go

Geoff (*to the Vicar*) Isn't it time you went?
Jane (*appalled*) Geoff!
Sarah He hasn't finished his coffee yet.
Vicar (*smiling politely*) I think it'll be cold by now.
Jane We'll make you some fresh.
Geoff No, you won't!
Sally Geoff!
Geoff He doesn't want any! Do you, Vicar?
Vicar Well, not if I have to wait for it in the cupboard.

Andrew, Jane and Sally look puzzled

Andrew I beg your pardon?
Sarah He was in the cupboard.
Andrew (*to Sarah, quietly*) *I* know he was in the cupboard. *You* know he was in the cupboard. Don't want the Vicar to know, do we?
Sarah But I *mean* the Vicar. *He* was in the cupboard.
Andrew What *are* you talking about?
Vicar It's very spacious.
Andrew What is?
Vicar The cupboard. Over there.
Andrew How do *you* know?
Sarah I told you. He was *in* the cupboard.
Andrew (*to the Vicar*) Were you?
Vicar Yes. But only for a moment.
Andrew When?
Vicar Just now. Your son put me in there.
Andrew (*outraged*) He's not my son!
Vicar Oh, dear me. I'm so sorry.
Andrew Nothing to be sorry about.
Vicar Well, whoever he is—he put me in.
Andrew He put you in the cupboard?
Vicar Yes. But not for long.

Andrew turns to the wall in despair

Sally Geoff, whatever's the matter with you?
Jane Yes. You really shouldn't go around putting people in cupboards.

Geoff I thought he'd be interested. A nice big cupboard like that. Just what he needs in the vestry.

Vicar (*who had not thought of that*) Yes! It would come in very handy. (*He turns to Andrew*) You see, the previous incumbent had far too many hymn books.

Geoff tries to urge the Vicar on his way

Geoff Right! Come on! And remember—don't take your hands off the handlebars!

Vicar What?

Geoff When you leave on your bicycle.

Vicar Why should I take my hands off the handlebars? I'm a vicar, not a circus performer. (*To Andrew*) He's the one who does the tricks, you know. (*He indicates Geoff*)

Andrew What tricks?

Vicar He did one for me just now when you were all out in the garden. Reaching up to heaven and walking backwards!

They all look at the Vicar in astonishment

Andrew I beg your pardon?

Vicar Both at the same time.

Andrew Reaching up to heaven?

Vicar Yes.

Andrew And walking backwards?

Vicar Yes.

Andrew Both at the same time?

Vicar Yes.

Andrew It doesn't sound quite like him, somehow.

Vicar (*to Geoff*) Go on. Why don't you show them?

Geoff (*embarrassed*) Well, I'd really rather not . . .

Vicar (*to Andrew*) It's very new. I'd never seen it before.

Andrew No, I'm sure you hadn't.

Jane (*puzzled*) Reaching up to heaven?

Sarah (*to Jane*) And walking backwards.

Jane Both at the same time?

Sarah Apparently . . .

Sally (*giggling*) Well, come on, Geoff! Show us your trick.

Vicar (*to Geoff*) Exactly as you did it for me.

Deeply embarrassed, Geoff slowly and reluctantly positions himself in front of the Vicar as he did before, raises his arms upwards and starts to walk slowly backwards. The Vicar smiles encouragingly. The others all watch in total amazement. They exchange astonished looks. Sally laughs. Geoff stops his performance and retreats in embarrassment. The Vicar turns to Andrew with a delighted smile

There! Isn't that splendid?

Andrew Well, it's better than planting cabbages.

The Vicar rises, preparing to leave

Vicar Well, it's been a great pleasure meeting you all. Perhaps I shall see you all on Sunday?
Andrew Why? What's happening *then*?

Jane pushes Andrew, then attempts to regain lost ground and make a good impression on the Vicar. She goes to him graciously

Jane Now, then, when would it be convenient for you to come and have tea with us? There are so many things to discuss, and coffee's been so dreadfully rushed this morning, hasn't it?
Vicar (*tentatively*) Well, actually, I—I don't have another appointment until after lunch . . .
Andrew (*enthusiastically*) Good! Then you'd better stay and have lunch here!

Jane turns to Andrew in alarm

Jane What?
Vicar Well, if you're quite sure. . . .

Geoff panics

Geoff He doesn't want lunch! Doesn't eat it! Do you, Vicar?
Sally (*moving hastily to Geoff*) Of course he wants lunch. Everybody wants lunch.
Geoff Well, he doesn't have to have it *here*, does he?

Somewhat bemused, the Vicar looks out of the window. Jane goes quickly to Andrew and speaks quietly and urgently

Jane Aren't you forgetting something?
Andrew You said you wanted to make a good impression. Now's your chance.
Jane But what about the one *out there*?
Andrew He won't be looking in the summer-house.
Jane He'd better not! (*She turns back to the Vicar and reassumes the smile of the polite hostess*) Perhaps another day would be more convenient?
Vicar Well, actually your husband's kind suggestion would suit me better. If that's all right with you . . .
Jane (*a little forced*) Yes—yes, of course! (*She gives Andrew a hard look*)
Geoff (*desperately*) But you've got your bicycle clips on! All ready to go!
Sally He can take them off! (*To the Vicar*) They do come off, don't they?

The Vicar smiles and takes off his bicycle clips with a flourish

Andrew Right! That's settled, then!
Vicar Well, it's very kind of you.

Andrew moves to the Vicar with a big smile

Andrew Not at all! You come and sit down over here, Vicar. (*He steers the Vicar enthusiastically back to sit on the sofa*) Make yourself at home. There we are. That's better, isn't it? Make yourself really comfortable. (*He sits beside the Vicar*) It was very decent of you to call on us, and now we've got you here we're certainly not going to let you get away!

Andrew and the others look at the Vicar, smiling hospitably: but Geoff, misunderstanding Andrew's intentions, is the picture of dreadful apprehension
Black-out

the CURTAIN *falls*

SCENE 2

The same. After lunch, the same day

A tray with coffee pot, milk jug, sugar and cups is on a table

Andrew is sitting comfortably on the sofa, sipping a cup of coffee. Jane comes in quickly from the hall, anxiously looking for someone. She comes down to the sofa

Jane Where is he?
Andrew Who?
Jane The Vicar!
Andrew I dunno. He was out there helping with the washing-up.
Jane Well, he's not there now.
Andrew I expect he had to go somewhere. Even Vicars have to go sometimes.
Jane You know, you really shouldn't have kept giving him wine all through lunch. The clergy aren't used to claret.
Andrew He could have refused. But every time I looked he'd got an empty glass again.
Jane Well, you didn't have to keep filling it up. And I can't think why you had to invite him to lunch today of all days.
Andrew He didn't give me much choice, did he? Anyhow, you're always telling me to mind my manners.
Jane Well, you chose a good day to do that with a dead body propped up in the summer-house. Who was he, by the way?
Andrew T.V. repair man.
Jane Oh no! What a pity. It's the last part of that thriller serial tonight. Now we shall *never* know who did it. How did it happen?
Andrew Faulty wiring, I suppose.
Jane You'd think they'd send a man who knew about electricity, wouldn't you?

Sarah comes in from the hall

Have you seen the Vicar?
Sarah Yes. He went for a walk in the garden.
Jane (*alarmed*) What?!

Sarah Said he felt like a breath of fresh air. I expect all that wine he drank at lunchtime made him a bit sleepy.

Jane Good heavens! He might go and look in the summer-house! Come along, Andrew! (*She tries to pull Andrew up from the sofa*)

Andrew Am I going somewhere?

Jane Of course you are! You're going to stop the Vicar.

Andrew But I was just having my coffee.

Jane The coffee can wait. (*She takes his cup and puts it down on the table*) We can't have the Vicar finding a dead man in the summer-house.

Andrew Serve him right if he does. Even parsons shouldn't go prying into people's private property.

Sarah But Andrew—think of the embarrassment.

Jane Besides, he'd think it very odd that we'd put him in the summer-house in the first place.

Andrew Well, it was your idea.

Jane Andrew—please! (*Reasonably*) All you've got to do is head him off. It's such a *little* thing to ask.

Andrew (*reluctantly*) Oh, all right. (*He starts to go*) But don't drink all the coffee.

Andrew goes out into the garden and trips over the suitcase

Oh, blast! (*Calling*) Vicar! I say, Vicar! Where the hell are you?

Andrew disappears down the garden

The telephone rings. Jane goes to answer it. Sarah sits on the sofa and pours coffee

Jane Hullo . . . Who? Yes, he's here. Just a minute. (*She puts down the receiver and goes towards the hall*) Someone for Geoff. (*She calls loudly as she approaches the archway*) Geoff! Teleph . . .!

Geoff comes in as she calls

Oh, there you are. Telephone for you.

Geoff (*puzzled*) For *me*?

Geoff goes and lifts the receiver tentatively. Jane joins Sarah

Hullo? (*Surprised*) . . . Oh, hullo, Dad. Where *are* you? . . . What are you doing there? . . . Oh, I see . . . What? . . . (*In sudden panic*) Now? Well, no—I'd rather you didn't! . . . No, of course not, but—one or two things have cropped up. I'd rather you put it off until another time . . . Yes, but . . . No, listen, I . . . Dad! Dad! Good heavens! (*His father has obviously hung up. He replaces the receiver, looking deeply troubled*)

Jane Is everything all right, Geoff?

Geoff (*distractedly*) What?

Sarah There's nothing wrong, is there?

Geoff Not exactly. That was my father. He's with my mother.

Jane Is that unusual?
Geoff In a call-box.
Jane In Stoke Poges?
Geoff Nearer than that. They'll be over here soon.
Sarah You mean they've taken up flying?
Geoff No, no—they're coming *here*! In the car.
Jane Coming here?
Geoff Yes.
Jane *Now?*
Geoff I'm afraid so! I did try to put them off, but Dad hung up on me so now I can't stop them.
Sarah Why should you want to stop them? It'll be lovely to meet your parents. And for them to meet us.
Geoff (*doubtfully*) Will it? Yes . . . Well, I'd better go and warn Sally. Oh, my God . . .!

Geoff stumbles out to the hall

Sarah You'd think he was ashamed of his parents or something.

Sarah and Jane get on with their coffee

Andrew appears in the garden with the Vicar

Andrew Can't have you trotting around the garden like that, Vicar. Not straight after lunch. You haven't had your coffee yet.
Vicar Oh, I don't think I could go through all that again!
Andrew I beg your pardon?
Vicar Coffee seems so complicated here.
Andrew Does it? I didn't know that.
Vicar You know, I must say—you've got a very nice garden.
Andrew Good of you to say so. Did you . . . did you see it *all*?
Vicar Oh, no.
Andrew Oh, good.
Vicar But enough to be going on with.

Andrew is not quite sure whether the Vicar intended this to be a loaded remark or not. He assumes a casual air

Andrew You . . . you saw the summer-house?
Vicar Oh, yes!
Andrew (*alarmed*) You *did*?
Vicar Yes. It's over there. Beyond the mulberry tree. Do you see? (*He takes Andrew a little way to show him*) Just over there.
Andrew Yes, Vicar. I *know* where it is.
Vicar Ah—yes. Of course. Silly of me. (*He goes and sits on the garden seat*)
Andrew It's . . . it's rather a nice summer-house. As summer-houses go.
Vicar Yes.
Andrew Very solid.
Vicar Yes.

Andrew Very . . . sunny.
Vicar Yes.

A pause

Andrew I often sit there.
Vicar In the summer-house?
Andrew Yes. It's so . . . peaceful.
Vicar Yes.
Andrew So I often sit there.
Vicar Yes.

A pause

Andrew After lunch, as a matter of fact. Just—(*he sits beside the Vicar*)—sit there.
Vicar After lunch?
Andrew Exactly. I contemplate. And I dream. It's my peaceful part of the day, just sitting in the . . .

Andrew ⎫ Summer-house ⎫ (*Speaking together*)
Vicar ⎭   ⎭

Andrew After lunch. So . . . Vicar . . . the chances are that during your stroll after the washing-up, you . . . may have seen someone in there.
Vicar In the summer-house?
Andrew Yes. It would have been me. Nobody else, you see. Just me. Sitting there. After lunch.
Vicar But I haven't been anywhere *near* the summer-house.

Andrew relaxes

Andrew Then why the hell didn't you *say* so?

A pause

Vicar I wonder if I might have a glass of water?
Andrew There's some coffee inside.
Vicar No, no. I would rather have a glass of water, if you don't mind.

Andrew rises

Andrew Yes, of course. Don't see why not. Right. (*He goes a little and then stops and looks back*) Glass of water?
Vicar Please.

Andrew returns to the Vicar

Andrew You going to show me a trick or something? You know—tumbler full of water upside down on the table, something of that nature?
Vicar Oh, no. It's for me. The wine was very nice but it does make one rather thirsty. (*He settles comfortably on the garden seat*)
Andrew Oh, I see. Right. Glass of water coming up. (*He starts to go again and trips over the bag*) Oh, blast! (*He goes inside*) Glass of water for the Vicar. (*He looks out into the garden*) Sorry about that, Vicar. (*He goes back inside*)

Sarah I've made coffee.
Andrew He doesn't fancy coffee. Prefers water. Got a bit thirsty after all
that wine.
Sarah And you can't do too much bicycling in this weather, you know.
(*She gets up*) I'll get it, Andrew.
Andrew Don't you worry, Sarah. I can see to it.
Sarah Well, Jane has got something to tell you.
Andrew Has she? Oh. That sounds ominous.

Sarah goes out into the hall

(*To Jane*) Well? What's it all about?
Jane (*urgently*) Geoff's parents!
Andrew What about them?
Jane They're not in Stoke Poges!
Andrew (*moving to the sofa*) Well, I expect they're allowed out occa-
sionally.
Jane They're coming *here*.
Andrew When?
Jane Now!

He sits beside her

Andrew *Now?*
Jane Yes. They rang from a call-box. They'll be here any moment! What
are we going to do?
Andrew Give them some coffee and a piece of cake.
Jane But what about the T.V. repair man?
Andrew *He* doesn't want any cake. He's in the summer-house.
Jane That's what I mean!
Andrew I don't expect they'll go in *there*.
Jane You can't be sure.
Andrew What do you expect *me* to do, then?
Jane You'll have to move him *out* of the summer-house just in case.
Andrew Don't be silly. There's nowhere else to put him. It's not our fault
if people can't take care of themselves.
Jane I know, darling, but I don't think Geoff's parents have to know all
about our bad luck on their first visit. It wouldn't be fair on Sally.
After all, she does want to make a good first impression on them. You'll
just have to keep them out of the garden.

*Sarah appears from the front of the house into the garden with a glass
of water for the Vicar*

Andrew On a day like this? That won't be easy.
Jane I know it's not easy, Andrew. You'll just have to do your best.

*Sarah peers at the Vicar, who is very still indeed, and comes into the house,
looking troubled*

Sarah Andrew . . .
Andrew Does he want some more water?
Sarah No. I don't think so. Andrew . . .

Andrew H'm?
Sarah I don't quite know how to put this, but . . .

Andrew and Jane both turn and look at Sarah apprehensively

Jane Sarah—what is it?
Sarah It's the Vicar . . . (*She puts the glass of water down on the table with finality*)

Andrew and Jane realize what has happened out in the garden

Andrew Oh, no . . .!
Jane He—he isn't . . .?

Sarah nods unhappily

He can't be!
Sarah He *is*!

A moment's stillness, then they all go quickly into the garden and gather around to look anxiously at the Vicar; The Vicar is sitting very still, his head lolling forward on his chest. Andrew takes a limp wrist and feels for the pulse. He straightens up gloomily and drops the Vicar's arm back into his lap

Andrew That's *all* we need. Well, our luck's certainly taken a turn for the worse, hasn't it?
Jane The Vicar hasn't exactly won the football pools!
Andrew What have we done to deserve this? Two in twenty-four hours!

Sally comes excitedly into the garden from the front of the house

Sally Have you heard the good news?
Andrew Good news? I didn't know there *was* any good news.

Sally sees the recumbent Vicar

Sally Oh. I thought he'd gone.
Andrew Who?
Sally The Vicar.
Andrew Don't talk to me about the Vicar!
Jane (*intervening quickly*) S'sh!
Andrew What?
Jane Don't disturb him! (*To Sally*) He's fast asleep.
Sally Really?
Jane Yes. Sleeping off his lunch.
Sarah I knew you shouldn't have given him all that wine, Andrew. He's not used to it.
Andrew He didn't drink as if he wasn't used to it.
Sally He certainly looks peaceful.
Andrew I'm not surprised.
Sally Is he going to be very long?
Andrew Who?
Sally The Vicar.

Andrew Very long where?
Sally Asleep.
Andrew Oh, yes. Years and years, I should think.
Jane (*to Sally*) Don't stare at him, darling! You'll wake him up.

Jane covers the Vicar's face with his hat. Andrew looks astounded, but holds his peace

Andrew (*to Sally*) What's this good news, then?
Sally Geoff's parents are coming!
Andrew I'd forgotten all about *them*!
Jane They're not here yet, are they?
Sally No, but they'll be arriving any minute.
Jane (*alarmed*) Will they?
Sally Yes. Isn't it *exciting*?
Andrew (*imitating her*) Oh, I can hardly control myself!

Sally gives him a look

Sally You will be nice to them, won't you?
Andrew Depends what they're like.
Jane Of course we will! We're looking forward to meeting them. Aren't we, Andrew?
Andrew Are we?
Sarah (*to Sally*) Hadn't you better go and wait for them?
Sally What?
Sarah Well, Geoff's alone out there, isn't he? And you know how nervous he gets. You ought to be with him when his parents arrive.
Jane Yes. You run along, Sally. We'll see to everything here.
Sally What about the Vicar?
Andrew Oh, I'll have him removed.
Sally What?
Jane (*quickly*) We'll wake him up and put him on his bicycle.
Sarah Yes. It's time he went and helped the Curate. Isn't it, Andrew?
Andrew Is it?

Jane hastily steers Sally towards the house

Jane So you and Geoff go and wait for his parents at the front door.
Sally Oh—all right, then.

Sally goes into the house, rather bewildered. She disappears into the hall

Jane returns to the others. Andrew moves above the seat and looks down at the Vicar

Andrew He's not going to be much help to the Curate like that, is he? What's the matter with you two?
Jane Well, we could hardly tell Sally the Vicar was dead just before she meets her future in-laws!
Sarah It seems such a pity that he had to die *now*.
Andrew Ah, well—that's life for you. Just as we thought our luck was changing, there's one out here, one in the summer-house and people

calling any minute. I'll go and phone the police. They can send an ambulance to pick him up. (*He starts to go*)

Jane Don't be silly, Andrew. Geoff's parents will be here any minute.

Andrew What's that got to do with it?

Jane Well, it won't create a very good impression on them if ambulances start screeching up the road the minute they arrive.

Andrew It'll create a worse impression if they find a dead vicar in the garden.

Sarah goes behind the seat to Andrew

Sarah Don't be silly, Andrew. We're not leaving him here.

Andrew Aren't we?

Jane Of course not. We'll put him in the summer-house.

Andrew That's already occupied.

Sarah There's plenty of room. We may as well put all our eggs in one basket.

Andrew Well, *I* think we should tell the police *now*.

Jane Please, Andrew! I don't want Geoff's parents to know anything about our accidents. It's so dreadfully embarrassing.

Sarah Yes. You must think of Sally and how she'd feel if they found out. You can ring the police when they've gone.

Andrew (*reluctantly*) I'll fetch the wheelbarrow. (*He starts to go up the garden but sees something and returns quickly*) Too late. They're here!

Jane Oh, no!

Andrew Well, there's a car stopping at the front door.

Jane Come on—inside, everybody! (*She starts to lead the others inside*)

Sarah But what about the Vicar?

Jane We'll keep them talking and Andrew will go and move him.

Andrew They'll see me through the window!

Jane Well, we can't leave him there, can we?

Andrew So what do we do?

Jane You'll think of something.

Andrew Oh, thank you very much!

They go inside

Geoff comes in from the hall

Geoff (*nervously*) They're here! (*Getting no reaction*) Shall I bring them in?

Andrew Unless you can think of anything *else* to do with them.

Geoff Right.

Geoff goes out to the hall again

Andrew Just think. If there was no T.V. and no church, none of this would be happening.

Geoff comes in from the hall with his mother. Audrey is about forty-eight, and rather tentative

Geoff This is my mother.

Andrew I'd never have guessed.

Jane (*quietly*) Andrew . . .!
Andrew Well, she's not very much like him, is she? (*To Audrey*) Are you?
Audrey Well—no. I—I suppose not. . . .
Andrew That's very lucky for you.
Jane (*quietly*) Will you behave?
Andrew It was meant as a compliment. She doesn't want to look like a man, does she? (*To Audrey*) You don't want to look like a man, do you? (*To Jane*) No, of course she doesn't. (*Full of charm he shakes hands with Audrey*) How do you do? I'm Sally's father. And this is her mother
Jane How do you do.
Audrey How do you do.
Andrew And this is my sister.
Sarah How do you do.
Audrey How do you do.
Andrew And this is your son.
Audrey (*turning to Geoff*) How do you . . .
Andrew Won't you sit down?
Audrey What a lovely garden!

Audrey heads for the garden, but Andrew takes her arm and guides her firmly back again

Andrew Never mind that.
Audrey But I *love* gardens.
Andrew Yes, I'm sure you do. But you can't go plunging about in it the minute you arrive. You'll ruin your shoes.
Jane I'll show you around later.
Audrey Oh, good. I shall enjoy that.
Andrew Take a seat.
Audrey Thank you.

Audrey starts for the window seat, but Andrew collects her once again and steers her to the sofa—and away from the window

Andrew Not over there—over here!

Audrey sits on the sofa

You'll find that much more comfortable.

They all settle. Jane on the window seat; Sarah on the armchair; Audrey on the sofa; Andrew stands by the sofa; Geoff hovers behind it

Well, now—tell me—how are things in Stoke Newington?

Audrey looks at him blankly

Audrey I beg your pardon?
Andrew Stoke Newington! What's it like living there?
Audrey (*bewildered*) I've no idea.
Andrew What?
Audrey We live in Stoke Poges.
Andrew I knew it was Stoke something-or-other. (*He goes to Geoff*) Is this the lot?

Geoff What do you mean?
Andrew You said your parents had arrived.
Geoff They have.
Andrew They usually come in twos. Don't tell me you couldn't muster one of each kind?
Geoff My father's outside.
Andrew What's he doing out there?
Audrey Edgar's seeing to the car.
Andrew Could have stayed at home and done that, couldn't he?

Edgar appears in the garden from the front of the house. He is a well-built man in his fifties, somewhat military in bearing. He notices the recumbent Vicar under the hat. Even for a military man this is a little surprising: but he shrugs it off and moves towards the house

Audrey He always likes to be one step ahead.
Jane (*alarmed*) Oh? Does he? (*She exchanges a look with Sarah*)
Audrey Yes. He says you should always be ready. You never know when you'll want to make a quick getaway.
Sarah (*quietly to Jane*) Yes. And the quicker the better . . .

Edgar comes in from the garden. They all look at him

Edgar Did you know that there's a vicar asleep in your garden?
Andrew Good lord, is he still there? (*He goes to look out of the window*)
Edgar Outside. Dead to the world.
Andrew Ah, yes. He wandered in last Wednesday.
Edgar Wednesday?
Andrew Early closing day. Wandered in and sat down out there. Must have been awfully tired. He's only woken up once since then. Once, that's all! Think of that. Once since Wednesday. Had two soft-boiled eggs and went straight off again.
Geoff (*abruptly*) This is my father!
Andrew We thought it might be. (*To Edgar*) How do you do.
Edgar How do you do.

Edgar and Andrew shake hands

Jane I'm Sally's mother.
Edgar How do you do.
Sarah And I'm Andrew's sister.
Edgar Who's Andrew?
Andrew I am.
Edgar Oh. How do you do.

Edgar and Andrew shake hands again

Sarah Don't take any notice of Andrew. He always exaggerates. The Vicar's been here for lunch.
Andrew And now he's sleeping it off.
Edgar Do you often have vicars asleep in the garden?

Andrew Why? Do you object to them?
Edgar No. Certainly not.
Andrew That's all right, then. You can sit down.
Edgar I've seen plenty of vicars in pulpits in my time. Never seen one in a garden before. (*He sits beside Audrey*)
Andrew Yes. I'm sorry. I'll get rid of him in a minute.
Jane Yes. You'll have to move him, Andrew.
Andrew I haven't had very much chance yet, have I?
Jane Well, *think* of something.
Andrew Think of something . . . (*He thinks of something and turns to the others suddenly*) Good lord! It really is hot today, isn't it? A real scorcher!

They look at him, rather surprised

Edgar Er—yes. Yes—very pleasant. (*He looks at Audrey and gives a little shrug*)
Andrew Too hot for *you*, is it?
Edgar Er—no. No, it's fine.
Andrew (*to Audrey*) How about you?
Audrey It's very pleasant.
Andrew Well, it's too hot for me. Whew! (*He loosens his shirt*)
Audrey Why don't we go and sit outside, then? I could look at the garden, too.
Andrew Too hot out there. Far too hot.
Audrey I love the heat.
Edgar So do I.
Andrew Well, we don't! No. Especially Jane. Far too hot for Jane. Jane burns very easily.
Edgar Who?
Andrew Jane. My wife.
Edgar Oh, yes. (*He turns to Sarah*) Too hot for you, is it?
Andrew No. No—wrong. That's my sister. *This* is my wife. She Jane. Me Tarzan. (*He emits a Tarzan cry and beats his chest*)

Jane and Sarah look at each other—Andrew really is going too far

Edgar And she burns?
Andrew What?
Edgar Your wife.
Andrew What about her?
Edgar She burns.
Andrew Burns? Oh, yes. Very easily. First day of spring and she turns bright pink.
Audrey (*to Jane*) Do you really?
Jane Oh, yes. Like a piece of litmus paper.
Audrey Good heavens!
Edgar *Ambre Solaire!*
Andrew Who?
Edgar That's what she needs. *Ambre Solaire*. We use it all the time.

Andrew Too late now. The shops are shut. I'll draw the curtains.
Edgar That sounds a little furtive.
Andrew It'll keep the room cool. Isn't that what they do in the tropics, Edgar?
Edgar Yes, but it's up in the nineties there.
Andrew Well, there's still time. I bet the mercury's climbing. Whew! Wow! Anyway, got to keep the sun off the furniture.

To the astonishment of everyone Andrew goes and draws the curtains, slightly reducing the light in the drawing-room area

There! That's better, isn't it?
Edgar (*puzzled*) It's *darker*, certainly.
Audrey (*disappointed*) You can't see the garden now.
Andrew (*delighted*) No. No, you can't, can you?

Jane and Sarah exchange a smile. So that is what he was up to

Now—how about a drink, Edgar? You'd like a drink, wouldn't you?
Edgar Well, I . . .
Audrey It's the middle of the afternoon.
Sarah I'll make some tea. (*She gets up and prepares to go*)
Andrew Good idea! I'll come with you. (*To Jane*) Darling, you give Edgar a drink. Whisky all right?
Edgar Well, it is only . . .
Andrew You're not teetotal, are you? Not on apple juice like him? No, of course not. Give him a whisky, Jane. And one for Geoff. He looks as if he could do with one. (*To Sarah*) Come along, Sarah! Tea!

Andrew and Sarah sweep off into the hall

Edgar and Audrey are finding the whole situation rather more than they can cope with. Geoff is totally stunned with embarrassment and apprehension. So it is left to Jane to attempt to carry it off and save the day. She moves towards them

Jane Geoff's told us all about you!

Edgar and Audrey look at her

Edgar Oh?
Jane Yes.

A pause

Edgar What?
Jane (*puzzled*) What?
Edgar What did he tell you about us?
Jane Er . . . he said that you live in Stoke Poges!

Edgar and Audrey exchange a look

You *do*, don't you?
Edgar Yes.
Jane Oh, good!

A pause

Edgar Is that *all* he told you about us?

Jane No. He said you were coming to visit us.

Edgar Ah . . .

Jane I'll get your whisky. (*She scuttles away quickly to pour the whisky*)

Sally comes in from the hall and reacts to the subdued light

Sally Why are you all sitting in the dark?

Jane It was your father's idea.

Sally But it's the middle of the afternoon. (*She goes to Geoff*)

Jane The sun was on the furniture. You know what he's like about furniture. There we are—whisky for you, Geoff—and whisky for you, Edgar. (*She gives the drinks to Geoff and Edgar*)

Geoff (*in a whisper to Sally*) Where have you been?

Sally (*also whispering*) Changing. You want me to look my best, don't you? (*Loudly*) You're drinking again!

Geoff Well—er . . .

Sally (*to Jane*) Shall I draw the curtains back? (*She goes towards the curtains*)

Jane (*rather too strongly*) No!!

They all look at her in surprise

Sally What?

Jane (*with a sweet smile*) Andrew wouldn't like it.

Sally But it's such a lovely day!

Audrey You don't want your mother to turn pink, though, do you?

Sally looks at her in surprise

Sally What?

Sally looks at Jane who hastily looks the other way

Geoff (*suddenly*) This is my father!

Sally Who?

Edgar I know it's hard to see me in this light but I'm over here. (*He raises his hand helpfully*)

Sally goes to him

Sally Oh—hullo. (*She shakes hands with him*)

Edgar (*approvingly*) H'm. Better than I expected.

Audrey You can't judge in this light, Edgar.

Edgar Cheers!

Edgar and Geoff drink

Outside, Andrew and Sarah come into the garden from the front of the house. Andrew is pulling a wheelbarrow

Andrew Come on, Sarah! We'll have to be quick. Can't keep those wretched parents in the dark too long.

Sarah Where are we going to put him?

Andrew In the summer-house for the time being. Now—you hold the wheelbarrow.

Sarah Right. (*She takes the wheelbarrow*)

Andrew Got a firm grip?

Sarah Yes.

Andrew We don't want him to go shooting off down the garden the minute we get him in. Right—here we go. (*He prepares to lift the Vicar*)

Inside, Edgar hears something

Edgar Did you hear something?

Sally Where?

Edgar Out in the garden. Thought I heard someone.

Jane (*quickly*) It'll be the gardener!

Sally I didn't know we'd got a gardener.

Jane moves anxiously towards the window

Jane He started yesterday. Small man in a big cap. (*To Audrey*) Awfully hard to get them, you know.

Audrey Big caps?

Jane Gardeners.

Edgar Let's have a look at him, eh? (*He rises and starts for the window*)

Jane No!

They all look at her in surprise

He's—he's very sensitive. Doesn't like being stared at. (*She steers Edgar back to the sofa*)

Sally You never mentioned a gardener yesterday.

Jane (*to Sally, sharply*) I forgot!

Edgar Wouldn't think you'd forget a sensitive gardener in a big cap who doesn't like being stared at.

Outside, Andrew is attempting to get a firm hold around the Vicar's waist before lifting him into the wheelbarrow

Andrew Good heavens, he weighs a ton!

Sarah Shall I help you?

Andrew No, Sarah. You hang on to the wheelbarrow. I'll manage in a minute.

Inside, Edgar again looks towards the garden

Edgar I'm sure I heard voices . . .

Jane Yes. He talks to himself!

Edgar A sensitive gardener in a big cap who talks to himself?

Jane Yes.

Edgar No wonder he doesn't like being stared at. Anyhow, there were *two* voices.

Sally (*to Jane*) We haven't got *two* gardeners, have we?

Jane I—I expect he brought a friend along.

Sally Geoff, go and have a look.
Jane No!

Before Jane can stop him, Geoff has reached the drawn curtains, parted them slightly and looked out. He freezes with horror at the sight of Andrew about to put the Vicar into the wheelbarrow. Andrew sees Geoff looking and freezes for a moment. Pause. Then Geoff closes the curtains quickly and holds on to them, his face white and set. He sits on the window seat in despair

Edgar See him?
Geoff (*stammering*) Wh-wh-wh-wh-wh-what?
Sally Geoff? Whatever's the matter?
Audrey He's gone quite white.
Edgar Did you see the gardener?
Geoff Yes. He's—he's getting rid of the rubbish.

Outside, Andrew succeeds in getting the Vicar into the wheelbarrow his legs hanging over one side. Andrew takes the Vicar by the feet and turns him round to a better position

Edgar What the hell's going on out there? (*He makes for the garden door purposefully*)
Jane No! No—wait a minute!

Edgar strides manfully out into the garden. He stops in surprise at the sight of Andrew with a wheelbarrow containing a vicar. Andrew and Sarah stand still for a moment. Then Andrew attempts to carry it off. He smiles broadly

Andrew Just giving him a ride around the garden.

Andrew goes off up the garden pushing the Vicar in the wheelbarrow. Sarah smiles sweetly at Edgar and follows Andrew

Edgar watches them go in astonishment. He turns slowly and comes unsteadily indoors, unable to believe what he has seen. He glances down at his whisky glass

Edgar That must have been a bloody strong whisky!
Audrey What's the matter, dear?
Edgar I think I must be seeing things . . .
Sally What did you see?
Edgar It was a—a . . . No, no, no! It couldn't have been!
Audrey What are you talking about?
Edgar Well—if I didn't know better I'd swear I saw a vicar sitting in a wheelbarrow.

Audrey is getting more and more bewildered. Geoff is in a daze. Sally puzzled. Jane anxious

Sally Why should the Vicar be in the wheelbarrow?
Edgar He was having a ride around the garden . . .!
Sally What?
Edgar Well, that's what your father said.
Audrey I thought he was making tea.

Jane Yes, of course he is! You must have been mistaken.

Edgar Ask *him*, then. (*Indicating Geoff*) He must have seen it, too.

Sally moves to Geoff

Sally Did you, Geoff?

Geoff (*dazed*) Sorry?

Sally When you looked out of the window—what did you see?

Jane He told you! The gardener!

Geoff (*weakly*) Yes. The gardener. Big man in a small cap.

Jane Small man in a big cap.

Geoff Small man in a big cap. Yes.

Jane (*to Edgar*) There you are. You were mistaken.

Edgar Well, we'll soon find out! (*He starts to make purposefully for the garden*)

At this moment Andrew and Sarah come in quickly from the hall with a tray of tea-things. Andrew is very breathless

Andrew Here we are then—tea!

Jane quickly moves the coffee tray and Andrew puts the tea down on the table. Sarah sits beside Audrey and attends to the tea

That didn't take long, did it?

Jane No, darling. You were *much* quicker than I expected.

Sally Daddy—may we have the curtains back? It's such a pity to miss the sunshine.

Andrew (*jovially*) Curtains? What curtains? Oh—the curtains! Yes, of course. Anything you like. Good idea. Let a bit of sun in. (*To Jane*) *You*'ll keep in the shade, though, won't you?

Sally draws back the curtains and the room is full of sunshine again

Now, Edgar—more whisky?

Edgar No fear! I mean—

Andrew Very strong stuff.

Edgar Yes. I know!

Sally (*at the window*) I say! He's gone!

Andrew Who?

Sally The Vicar. He was out there asleep.

Andrew Ah. Yes. He hoped you wouldn't mind if he didn't stay for tea, but he had to go. He was awfully sorry because he'd love to have met you, Edgar. And you, too, Audrey. He'd have loved that. But he had to go. You know the clergy. A vicar rarely has an easy ride.

Edgar Not even in a wheelbarrow?

Andrew What?

Sarah intervenes with tea

Sarah A cup of tea!

Audrey Oh, thank you. I could do with one. (*She takes a cup*)

Sarah Sally?

Sally No, thanks. (*She sits next to Geoff*)

Sarah Jane?
Jane Lovely! (*She takes a cup from Sarah and sits on the armchair*)
Sarah Andrew?
Andrew No, thank you, Sarah. I've only just had my coffee.
Edgar (*to Andrew*) Did he enjoy it?
Andrew Who?
Edgar The Vicar! The ride in the wheelbarrow!
Andrew (*calmly*) Difficult to say. You know the clergy. Not very demonstrative.
Audrey (*surprised*) You mean the Vicar really *was* in the wheelbarrow?
Andrew Oh, yes.
Edgar There you are! What did I tell you?
Sally But *why* was he in the wheelbarrow?
Andrew Why? (*Thoughtfully*) Well—I went out into the garden, you see. Because that's where he was. In the garden. Sleeping. After lunch. What a nice lunch it was, wasn't it? Fresh vegetables, horseradish sauce . . .
Sally (*firmly*) Go on, Daddy.
Andrew Yes. Right. Well, I thought he might like a cup of tea. You see? As we were making tea, I thought—only polite—ask the Vicar if he'd like one.
Sally So what happened?
Andrew Well—I woke him up. Because he was asleep, you see. And I said, "Vicar," I said, "would you like a cup of tea?"
Audrey That was very considerate of you.
Andrew Oh, thank you. Audrey. *I* thought so, too. But then I've always been like that. Even as a small boy. Always put other people first. Especially people in pulpits.
Sally (*persisting*) What did *he* say?
Andrew Say? Well—he looked at me for a moment. About five or six seconds it was. And then he said—and you're going to find this very difficult to believe—he said, "Would you mind giving me a ride in the wheelbarrow?"
Edgar I think I *will* have another whisky!
Andrew Help yourself.

Edgar helps himself

Sally So what did *you* say?
Andrew What *could* I say? If a vicar asks for a ride in a wheelbarrow, how can you refuse?
Edgar What about the gardener?
Andrew (*blankly*) What gardener?
Jane *Our* gardener, darling!

Andrew looks at her blankly

The new one. You remember!
Andrew No . . .
Geoff (*muttering*) Small man in a big cap . . .

Andrew (*getting the message*) Small man in a big cap? Ah! Is he out there now?

Jane Yes, he *is*!

Andrew Well, I didn't give *him* a ride. Didn't ask for one. So he didn't get one. First come, first served, eh, Edgar?

Sally Where is he now?

Andrew Pruning the roses.

Sally The Vicar!

Andrew Oh, the Vicar. On his way back to the vicarage. Went racing off on his bike. Bit too fast for my liking. Very reckless, the clergy.

Audrey Can I have a look in the garden now?

Andrew Oh, you still want to do that?

Audrey Yes. I love gardens!

Jane rises apprehensively and gives her cup to Sarah

Jane Wouldn't you rather see the bathroom?

Audrey Oh, no.

Jane Kitchen? Very nice kitchen. High level grill, all that sort of thing.

Audrey rises

Audrey I'd prefer to see the garden.

Andrew Right! Sarah, you're very fond of flowers. Perhaps *you'd* show her around the garden?

Sarah (*rising*) Of course. I'd be delighted. (*To Audrey*) Right. Off we go, then!

Sarah and Audrey start to go into the garden

Audrey By the way, do you have a summer-house?

Andrew (*loudly*) No!

Sally Of course we have, Daddy.

Andrew Of course we have, Daddy . . .

Andrew follows them into the garden. Sarah is moving below the garden seat. Audrey hangs back a little as Andrew comes out

Audrey I'm sure I saw a summer-house as we drove in. The other side of the mulberry tree.

Andrew But it's very small. Hardly worth a glance.

Audrey (*moving to Sarah*) But I love summer-houses of *every* size.

Andrew Yes, you would!

Sarah It's not very convenient, though, is it, Andrew?

Andrew moves quickly to Audrey

Andrew No—no, it isn't! It's very *in*convenient.

Jane and Edgar come out into the garden

Audrey What do you mean?

Andrew It's the gardener. He's cleaning it out.

Audrey You said he was pruning the roses.

Andrew That was before. He *was* cleaning the roses, now he's pruning the summer-house. Garden chairs and croquet mallets all over the place.

Audrey (*ecstatically*) How lovely! I must see it all!

Edgar She won't leave without seeing every inch of the garden, you know.

Andrew Won't she? Oh. (*To Sarah*) You'd better make a start, then. (*Pointedly*) Down the *far* end is the nicest, I think. And I'll go and tell the gardener to finish off quickly and then you can see the summer-house.

Sarah and Audrey head for the exit to the pond

Sarah (*as they go*) Come along, then, Audrey. Let's start with the del-phiniums.

Audrey (*seeing Geoff's bag*) I'm sure that's *Geoff*'s bag over there.

Sarah Oh—that. Yes, it is.

Audrey You shouldn't let him leave it out here. Somebody could have a nasty accident.

Audrey and Sarah go off down the garden

Andrew turns and laughs loudly at Edgar, who reacts away nervously and almost trips over Geoff's bag. His momentum and loss of balance propel him rapidly into the house again where he sits with a thump on the sofa. Sally rises in surprise and looks at him. Outside, Andrew takes Jane aside slightly and speaks urgently

Andrew Get them out of there!

Jane What?

Andrew They'll see me through the window.

Jane How am I supposed to get them out of there?

Andrew gives her a triumphant smile, getting his own back

Andrew You'll think of something.

Andrew goes quickly up the garden and disappears

Jane thinks of something and goes into the house

Jane (*brightly*) Sally! Why don't you show Geoff's father over the house?

Sally and Edgar look at her in surprise

Sally Why? He doesn't want to buy it, does he?

Jane (*persisting*) He'd be *interested*. (*To Edgar*) Wouldn't you, Edgar?

Edgar Well, I . . .

Jane Of course you would! It's a very nice house!

Edgar Yes, I'm sure it is, but . . .

Jane (*a little too strongly*) Then go and look at it! (*She turns to Sally with a big smile*) You can start with the airing cupboard.

Sally (*bemused*) Oh—all right. If it means so much to you . . . (*She starts to go*)

Edgar (*rising without enthusiasm*) Yes. I'm sure it'll be lovely.

Sally gives Jane a puzzled look and goes out with Edgar into the hall

Geoff is still on the window seat, dazed and beaten like a camel with a load of straw. Jane turns to him urgently

Jane Now, Geoff—why don't you just . . .?

Geoff gets up and moves towards her, appalled

Geoff You *did* it, didn't you?

Jane Did what?

Geoff You said you would and you did . . .!

Jane Sorry?

Geoff Where did you put him?

Jane Oh, the man in the pond? Well, we put him in the summer-house. We thought we'd see to all that after your parents had gone. They don't want to talk about things like that. Not on their first visit. (*She goes and looks anxiously out of the window*)

Geoff (*loudly*) I wasn't talking about the man in the pond!

Jean You really must try not to get so excited. It's awfully bad for the liver. Would you like to go with the others and look at the airing cupboard.

Geoff (*wildly*) Did you put the *Vicar* in the summer-house as well?

Jane What are you talking about. The Vicar went home on his bicycle.

Geoff I *saw* him! He was sitting in the wheelbarrow and he was dead!

Jane Of course he wasn't dead. He was just having a ride.

Geoff You said he'd die if he came here and he did!

Jane gives an anxious look towards the garden, then pretends to be ill

Jane Ooooh! Oh, dear! Oh—I—I suddenly feel rather faint . . .

Geoff hovers ineffectually

Geoff Can I get you something? Whatever's the matter?

Jane I expect it's the sun.

Geoff The sun?

Jane I can't stand too much sun, you see. I'll have to draw the curtains again. You don't mind, do you? (*She quickly draws the curtains and the room becomes slightly darker.*) There. Oh, there we are. That's much better.

Geoff Can I get you some water?

Jane No. I'll be all right in a minute. (*She goes to the sofa and lies down*)

Geoff A—a brandy?

Jane What a good idea! I think there's some out in the kitchen.

Geoff I saw some over here. (*He looks amongst the drinks*)

Jane (*firmly*) No, Geoff. In the kitchen.

Geoff Oh. Right. Shan't be a minute.

Geoff goes out into the hall

Jane gets up quickly, races to the garden door and looks out

Andrew returns furtively from up the garden

Jane (*urgently*) Well? Have you done it yet?

Andrew Give me a chance. He's round the corner. Just wanted to make sure the coast was clear.

Jane Well, I've got rid of Edgar and drawn the curtains, but you'll have to be quick!

Andrew Right.

Jane Where are you going to take him?

Andrew I thought I'd put him on the compost heap.

Andrew retires quickly up the garden

Jane races back inside and resumes her position on the sofa, only with her head at the opposite end

Geoff returns with a glass of brandy

Geoff Here you are. (*He brings the brandy to where her head had been but only finds her feet. He reacts, then takes the brandy around to her*)

Jane Oh, thank you, Geoff. (*She takes it in true invalid fashion*)

Geoff I think I'll get my mother. She's awfully good at illness. (*He starts to go towards the garden door*)

Jane No!!

Geoff What? (*He returns to her*)

Jane (*quickly remembering to be frail*) Please don't leave me. I'll be all right in a minute. But I don't want to be alone. (*She takes another sip of brandy and puts the glass down on the sofa table*)

Geoff (*hovering anxiously*) I think I'd *better* fetch my mother . . .

Jane No—stay here!

She grabs him to prevent him leaving. He loses his balance and falls across her on the sofa

At this moment Sally and Edgar return from the hall and see them in what appears to be a rather compromising position on the sofa

Sally Mother!!

Geoff leaps up in fright

What on earth are you doing?

Jane (*sitting up*) I felt a little faint. Geoff was helping me.

Sally In the dark?

Jane (*weakly*) Such bright sunshine . . .

Sally (*rather tartly*) You lie in it for hours in the South of France.

Jane That's different. You two were very quick. You must have gone round the house at the double.

Edgar (*to Jane*) Are you feeling all right now?

Jane Yes, thank you. I'm better now I've had some brandy.

Geoff Can I draw back the curtains, then?

Jane Er—well—yes. (*Anxiously*) I—I *think* so. It *should* be all clear by now.

Geoff draws back the curtains and the sunshine floods back into the room

*Andrew appears from up the garden with the Vicar in the wheelbarrow.
He puts the barrow down for a moment to get his breath*

Geoff gazes in horror at what he sees

Geoff (*pointing wildly*) Aaah! There he is, you see! There's the Vicar! Out
there!
Sally What?
Geoff Right! That settles it!

Geoff goes off determinedly to the hall

Sally Whatever's the matter? Geoff! Geoff!

Sally runs off after Geoff

Jane goes quickly out into the garden. Edgar starts to follow

Jane (*to Andrew*) I thought you'd have done it by now!
Andrew I was going as fast as I could. He's very heavy for a vicar.

*Edgar comes out into the garden. Andrew hastily covers the Vicar's face
with his handkerchief*

Edgar Taking the Vicar for another ride?
Andrew Oh, no. This is the gardener. It's *his* turn now.

Andrew goes off down the garden with the wheelbarrow

*Edgar looks shattered. He goes to the garden chair and sinks on to it. Jane
smiles sweetly*

Jane Andrew is *so* full of fun, isn't he?
Edgar (*grimly*) I suppose you *could* call it that.
Jane It's so exciting having such a large garden. You never know what
you're going to find next, do you?

*Audrey and Sarah come in from down the garden. Audrey is looking back
the way they came. Sarah is trying to urge her on*

Sarah No, no. I'm sure you were mistaken. That wasn't Andrew.
Audrey Looked just like him.
Sarah No. I expect it was the gardener.
Edgar Yes, it was . . .
Sarah Ah! You saw him, too?
Edgar Yes. He just went by.
Sarah (*to Audrey*) There you are, you see. Walking along pushing the
wheelbarrow.
Edgar No. Riding along *in* the wheelbarrow.
Audrey What?
Edgar The gardener was in the wheelbarrow. At least, Andrew *said* it was
the gardener.
Audrey In the wheelbarrow?
Jane (*quickly*) Did you enjoy the garden?
Audrey Yes. It's beautiful. (*She looks pointedly at Sarah*) But I still haven't
seen the summer-house.

Sarah Ah. No. You haven't, have you? (*Suddenly*) I shall go and do the washing-up.

Jane looks at her in surprise

Jane What?
Sarah (*with a big smile*) The washing-up!
Jane (*puzzled*) Oh—all right, Sarah. If you want to.
Sarah I shan't be long.

Sarah goes inside

(*To Audrey*) Sarah's always *so* helpful in the house.

Inside, Sarah almost collides with Sally, who is coming in briskly. She goes off into the hall. Sally is looking rather upset

Sally (*calling loudly*) Mummy!
Jane Good heavens! Excuse me a minute.

Jane goes inside. Edgar and Audrey remain sitting dazedly in the sunshine

Edgar *I*'ve never had a ride in a wheelbarrow . . .
Audrey The delphiniums are beautiful.
Edgar What?
Audrey Delphiniums.
Edgar (*uninterested*) Oh, yes . . .
Sally (*inside the house, unhappily*) It's true, isn't it?
Jane What's true?
Sally About the Vicar. (*She sits miserably on the sofa*)
Jane (*vaguely*) I don't know what you mean.
Sally I thought he was very still for a man who was only asleep! It would happen *today*, wouldn't it? Just when Geoff's parents are here. . . .
Jane (*sympathetically*) Oh, darling, you mustn't worry. (*She sits beside Sally and comforts her*)

Outside, Andrew appears from down the garden with an empty wheelbarrow

Edgar looks up from his reverie

Edgar (*to Andrew*) Fell out, did he?
Andrew H'm? What?
Edgar The gardener! Did he fall out?

Andrew puts down the wheelbarrow thoughtfully

Andrew Well—he didn't exactly *fall* out. He *got* out. I said to him—I said, "Now, look here, Fred—I simply cannot face the return journey with you in this wheelbarrow". So he got out. Good as gold. He's on the compost heap now.

Andrew picks up the wheelbarrow and trundles it off up the garden

Audrey I don't think I want to stay here much longer.
Edgar Nor do I. They're all as mad as hatters.

Sally (*inside the house*) It's just such rotten bad luck!
Jane I know, darling. I tell you what—we'll move from here. Sell up, buy
a lovely new house, and start all over again.
Sally (*brightening*) You mean it?
Jane Of course I mean it. You don't think your father and I want to stay
on here after all this, do you?
Sally Oh, good! (*She embraces Jane quickly*) I'll go and tell Geoff. (*She
starts to go*)
Jane What's he doing out there?
Sally Telephoning the police.
Jane Surely he could have left that until after his parents had gone?
Sally That's what *I* told him.

Sally goes out into the hall

*Jane rises and heads for the garden. Outside, Edgar and Audrey are sitting
glumly, then Edgar gets up*

Edgar Well? You ready, then?
Audrey Ready?
Edgar For the off!
Audrey (*erupting suddenly*) Edgar, there's no need to shout.

Audrey gets up as Jane comes out of the house

Jane I'm so sorry. We seem to be neglecting you dreadfully. I expect
you're longing to see the rest of the garden.
Edgar No!
Jane What?
Edgar We've got to go.
Jane *Now?*
Edgar Yes.
Jane Oh, what a shame.
Edgar Better make a start.

Andrew appears from up the garden. He is looking a trifle puzzled

Jane goes to him

Jane Geoff's parents are leaving, darling. Isn't that a shame?
Andrew (*miles away*) What?
Audrey I'll get my bag. (*She goes inside to get her handbag from the sofa*)
Edgar (*calling after her*) Well, don't take too long about it! (*He lingers
just inside the garden door*)

Andrew takes Jane aside a little and whispers urgently

Andrew I can't find him!
Jane Who?
Andrew The one up there.
Jane The Vicar?
Andrew No, no. The Vicar's down there! The T.V. repair man was in the
summer-house—and now he isn't!

Jane Then where is he?
Andrew *I* dunno! I went to move him out and he'd gone.

Audrey and Edgar return to the garden

Edgar Right! We'll be off, then.
Andrew Off? Aren't you going to look in the summer-house?
Edgar I'm afraid not.
Andrew You mean we've been to all this trouble and now you're not even going to *look* at it?
Edgar Another time, perhaps.
Audrey Edgar, perhaps we could just have a quick look at the summer-house . . .
Edgar Never mind the bloody summer-house! Come *on*!

Edgar drags Audrey off up the garden

Jane and Andrew watch them go in astonishment

Jane Well . . .!
Andrew What an extraordinary way to behave!
Jane Pity they didn't go sooner. Would have saved you all that rushing about, darling

They laugh

Andrew Well, I'd better go and telephone the police.
Jane I think Geoff's already done that.
Andrew Really? Oh, good. (*He sits on the garden seat*)

Sally comes running in from up the garden

Sally Geoff's parents!
Andrew Good lord. They're not coming back, are they?
Sally No. They've gone! I saw them leaving.
Jane Yes. They seemed in a hurry to get back to Stoke Poges. (*She sits on the seat beside Andrew*)
Sally (*quite put out*) But they didn't even say goodbye! What a very rude way to behave. (*She sits on the arm of the garden seat*)

Sarah comes in from up the garden

Sarah Did I hear a car?
Andrew Yes. Edgar and Audrey have gone.
Sarah Gone?
Andrew Yes.

Sarah is rather annoyed at this

Sarah Oh. I could have saved myself the trouble, then. (*She sits on the garden chair*)
Jane What trouble?
Sarah Well—the T.V. repair man. I've been moving him in the other wheelbarrow.

Andrew Ah, so it was you! I wondered where he'd got to.
Jane Where did you put him?
Sarah Well, I thought the safest place was in the boot of your car Andrew.
Andrew What a good idea! I never thought of that. (*He chuckles*)
Sarah He looks really cosy, I must say. I covered him up with your lovely travelling-rug.

A pause

Andrew What lovely travelling-rug?
Sarah The red and green one in the boot of your car.

A pause

Andrew Which car did you put him in?
Sarah Your red saloon, of course.

Andrew starts to laugh

Andrew Sarah—the red saloon belongs to Edgar!

They all react

Sarah What? You don't mean . . .?
Andrew Yes! Edgar and Audrey have got a passenger!

They all laugh uproariously

Can you imagine Edgar's face when he opens the boot? I'd like to see him trying to explain *that* one away!

They laugh louder

Geoff comes in from the hall. He is looking rather sheepish. He joins them in the garden

Geoff Constable Burgoyne is in the hall.
Andrew Oh, splendid! You better bring him out here.
Geoff I told him about the Vicar and the T.V. repair man—·
Andrew Good.
Geoff —(*awkwardly*) and . . . he told *me* all about the others.

They all look puzzled

Andrew What do you mean?
Sally You already *knew* about the others.
Jane Yes. We told you last night.
Geoff (*embarrassed*) Yes. But you see—I thought that—I didn't realize that . . . that they'd all been . . . accidental.
Andrew Whatever *did* you think, then?
Geoff Well, I thought that—that—well, that you had all been . . . (*He peters out with a nervous gesture*)
Andrew You didn't think that we had all been . . . ? (*He repeats Geoff's gesture*) Did you hear that, darling? He thought that we had all been . . . (*He does the gesture again*) No wonder he was dashing about like a frightened rabbit!

Sally Honestly, Geoff! You are stupid!

They all enjoy the situation enormously. Geoff tries to overcome his shame and join in the general merriment

Geoff Yes—yes, I am, aren't I? I just misunderstood, you see!

Andrew (*through his chuckles*) Anyhow, the constable's talked to you and now you're convinced?

Geoff Yes—yes, of course!

Andrew Good. Good. It's nice to know you're convinced. (*To Jane*) It's nice to know he's convinced, isn't it, darling?

Jane It certainly is!

They laugh. But a tiny doubt returns to Geoff

Geoff Shouldn't I be?

Andrew (*vaguely*) What?

Geoff Shouldn't I be convinced?

Andrew (*evasively*) Well—that's up to you, isn't it? Entirely up to you.

Geoff is getting nervous again

Geoff Wh-what do you mean?

Andrew No, no, no. If you're satisfied, that's fine.

Jane, Sarah and Sally are trying hard to keep their faces straight

Geoff I don't know what you mean. They—they *were* all accidents, weren't they?

Andrew smiles enigmatically

Andrew What do *you* think?

Geoff does not know what to think. He looks at Sarah, then uncertainly back at Andrew and the others. They all start to laugh at his discomfort, as the Lights fade to a Black-out, and—

the CURTAIN *falls*

FURNITURE AND PROPERTY LIST

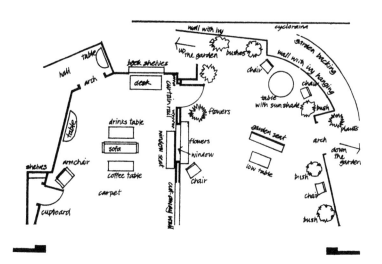

ACT I

SCENE 1

On stage: **DRAWING ROOM:**
Sofa
Coffee table
Armchair
Desk
Drinks table. *On it:* bottle of gin, bottle of sherry, bottle of brandy, 2 decanters of whisky, tonic water, empty soda syphon, ice-bucket with ice, various glasses
Bookshelves with books

GARDEN:
Wicker garden seat
Glass-topped table
Wicker armchair
Ladder
Bucket of water
Wash leather

Off stage: Rubber gloves **(Jane)**
Briefcase **(Andrew)**
Evening newspaper **(Andrew)**
Weekend bag **(Geoff)**
Soda syphon (in cupboard)
Handbag **(Sally)**
Morning paper **(Andrew)**
Bag with shopping **(Jane)**
Handbag **(Jane)**
Red wellington boots **(Jane)**
Yellow wellington boots **(Sally)**

Personal: **Vicar:** bicycle clips

SCENE 2

Strike: Ladder
Bucket
Rubber gloves
Wash leather
Used glasses

Re-set: **Geoff's** bag

ACT II

SCENE 1

Off stage: Wheelbarrow **(Andrew)**
Cup of coffee **(Sarah)**

SCENE 2

Set: Tray on coffee table. *On it:* coffee pot, milk jug, sugar bowl, 4 coffee cups and saucers, spoons

Off stage: Glass of water **(Sarah)**
Handbag **(Audrey)**
Tea-tray. *On it:* teapot, milk jug, 4 teacups and saucers, teaspoons **(Andrew)**
Glass of brandy **(Geoff)**

Personal: **Vicar:** handkerchief
Audrey: handbag

LIGHTING PLOT

Property fittings required: nil

A drawing-room and garden. The same scene throughout

ACT I, SCENE 1 A summer evening

To open: Warm evening sunshine

Cue 1   **Andrew:** "You look as if you've seen a ghost."   (Page 27)
        Black-out

ACT I, SCENE 2 A summer day

To open: Bright summer sunshine

Cue 2   **Geoff:** "What the hell are *you* doing here?"   (Page 40)
        Black-out

ACT 2, SCENE 1 A summer day

To open: Bright summer sunshine

Cue 3   **Andrew:** "... we're certainly not going to let you get away!"   (Page 54)
        Black-out

ACT 2, SCENE 2 A summer day

To open: Bright summer sunshine

Cue 4   **Andrew** draws the curtains   (Page 65)
        Decrease light in drawing-room area

Cue 5   **Geoff** slightly parts curtains   (Page 68)
        Slightly increase light in drawing-room area

Cue 6   **Geoff** closes curtains   (Page 68)
        Reverse Cue 5

Cue 7   **Sally** draws back the curtains   (Page 69)
        Reverse Cue 4

Cue 8   **Jane** draws the curtains   (Page 73)
        Same as Cue 4

Cue 9   **Geoff** draws back the curtains   (Page 74)
        Reverse Cue 4

Cue 10 **General laughter**   (Page 80)
        Fade to Black-out

EFFECTS PLOT

ACT I

SCENE 1

Cue 1　As CURTAIN rises　　　　　　　　　　　　　(Page 1)
　　　　　Faint birdsong in garden

SCENE 2

Cue 2　As CURTAIN rises　　　　　　　　　　　　(Page 27)
　　　　　Faint birdsong in garden

Cue 3　Sarah: "... go and see it next door..."　　　(Page 39)
　　　　　Front doorbell rings

ACT II

SCENE 1

No cues

SCENE 2

Cue 4　**Andrew** exits　　　　　　　　　　　　　(Page 55)
　　　　　Telephone rings